News To Me

News To Me

REMEMBRANCES OF A TEXAS NEWSWOMAN

Juliet K. Wenger

with Audrey Ellzey

EAKIN PRESS Austin, Texas

FIRST EDITION
Copyright © 2001
By Juliet K. Wenger
Published in the United States of America
By Eakin Press
A Division of Sunbelt Media, Inc.
P.O. Drawer 90159 ⌂ Austin, Texas 78709-0159
email: eakinpub@sig.net
⌂ website: www.eakinpress.com ⌂
ALL RIGHTS RESERVED.
1 2 3 4 5 6 7 8 9
1-57168-500-6 HB
1-57168-518-9 PB

For CIP information, please access:
www.loc.gov

Dedication

A fisherman built a new boat, board by board, on the shore of Ingleside Cove. Each day after school, one neighborhood child after another would stop by, watch awhile, then ask, "What are you going to name her?"

To each he gave the same reply: "I'm going to name her after you." The day the boat was launched, the children crowded around eagerly to see which name was painted on the transom. The name was *After You*.

As I wrote this story, word by word, each of my best of friends came to mind. They made my life abundant.

Mary Splawn Taylor, Frances Lee Dunn, and Lucille Luby from my childhood; Barbara Timon and Phyllis Boyd over most of a lifetime; Nancy Heard, her daughters, Sara and Melissa, and their husbands, Brian and James. Kathleen Jester Duffy, whose daughter, Susan, is my goddaughter, and her husband, Steven, and godchildren Michael Yankee, Loren and Geoffrey Moran, and Taylor Dudley and Ellen Yankee, like my godchildren and their families, are part of my heart. Marg Brown for thirty years. Miki McElroy. Later in life, Claudia Jackson, JoAnn Luckie, Jane and Cal Goode, Helon Howard, Mary McAdam, Florence and Jack Wyatt, Bettye and Hugh Ledford, Sandy and Dennis McGill, Chuck and Betty Shamel, Bonnie Lou Prouty, and Sandra and Tom Taylor.

Anna Ramsey, Linda Pugh, Corie McGill, and Hughie Fischer, my neighborhood children, taught me delight.

My own family has been precious to me. My grandmother, Juliet Taylor Thompson; my mother, Sue Taylor Thompson Knight; my father, Launcelot Mayes Knight; my aunt and uncle, Juliet and Perry Tucker; their daughters, Juliet Bell Dudley and Susan Yankee, and their husbands, Phil and Dick; my father's brother, Hugh Knight, and his wife, Fanny, who took time to write hundreds of letters and one book, chapter by chapter, to pass on to me what life had taught them. Their children and grandchildren lived at a distance but also remained close to me. My husband, Chris, came into my life and became my life.

Vann, Mary, and Kathleen Kennedy have become family to me, always there, considerate, loving. I can't imagine life without them.

Thanks to Jennie, Fran, and Millie, and to Leigh Anthony. Many thanks also to the news staff that worked with me when we were pacesetters in Texas radio and television. They gave me that most exhilarating experience of teaming up with exceptional people.

Bill Allen's really to blame for the book. Professor emeritus of creative writing at the University of Ohio but Texan first and always, he suggested I write a book of essays on the sort of things that every reporter sticks in the back of her mind to write someday when she has time. When he was in South Texas writing the book *Aransas* with Sue Taylor, he would guide me in writing *News to Me*. Who could resist? Bill is an author, Pulitzer Prize nominee, and the best of teachers, the kind who always convinces you that an essay you have finished writing is deathless prose, immediately before he sends you home to rewrite every word of it.

When I thought the manuscript was finished, Audrey Ellzey joined our team as editor. She brought to the endeavor a mind sharp as a cactus thorn, and with her vision and intensity of determination to achieve excellence, widened my vision. The abilities of Bill and Marjorie Walraven were important in bringing the book together, and anyway it is so much fun to be with them. Thank you also to Virginia Messer, Angela Buckley, and Michelle Dudro for their work on the book.

To each in turn, I said as I wrote, "This I dedicate to you." And so I do.

—Juliet Knight Wenger

Contents

Foreword by Bill Walraven	vii
1. Landing a Job	1
2. Jailhouse Tête-à-Tête	7
3. One of God's Strays	10
4. The Iconoclasts	14
5. Nothing is Forever	18
6. So This is War	22
7. Sweet and Sour Justice	25
8. A Short Flight	29
9. Law and Disorder	33
10. On the Night Side	38
11. Old Ways and New	45
12. McCracken and Mulvany	48
13. Rob's World	54
14. Progress Be Damned	59
15. Downriver	63
16. Wavelengths	68
17. Sky High	71
18. Sound of the Siren	75
19. The Oil Editor	81
20. The FCC Hearing	86
21. Lights, Camera, Action	91

22. A Genius and a Gentleman	97
23. Only the Best	104
24. Delinquent Parents	109
25. Embattled Empire	113
26. The Beltway	119
27. Setting Sail	122
28. The Oilman and the Skipper	126
29. And Then There Was Celia	132
30. Guarding the Turf	138
31. Integrity and Power	143
32. Ancestral Grounds	149
33. Forgive Us Our Differences	155
34. The Onion King	159
35. Transitions	168
36. Women at the Helm	172
37. The Scotties	175
38. The Gift of Sight	183
39. Coming Full Circle	186

Foreword

Robert M. Jackson, editor of the *Corpus Christi Caller-Times*, was a close observer of Juliet Knight Wenger's news reporting on KSIX radio and KZTV. Apparently, he never missed a newscast.

I knew this because he listened to the noon news during his lunch hour. He came back to the office and compared the contents of the afternoon *Times* to what he had heard. He often yelled to ask me why I didn't have something Judy had reported. He did the same thing when I worked on the *Caller*.

There wasn't much I could say. She beat me again. But I learned from her how to be a police reporter: I rode with the cops at night, sat with detectives on stakeouts, took statements from prisoners, and generally made myself useful. I learned never to betray a confidence and never jump the gun with a release that would blow a case, and I made sure I never broke my word.

That was a start. Then, every now and then I had her on the run, but Judy had grown up in this town, and she had contacts, both high and low. And a reporter is only as good as his—or her—contacts.

In time, I was about even with her on police coverage, but that was only a small part of her job. She was also keeping up with the flow of news from city hall, the courthouse, the federal building, and other sources of news. In competition with a veteran staff at the newspaper, she was more than holding her own.

I learned never to gloat over a minor scoop. Mr. Jackson

would fuss at me about a story I missed. It was usually too late to point out to him that Judy had waited a day or two and come back with a new lead on a story I had previously reported. She was so skilled, it looked for all the world like a new story.

The rivalry was never personal. No animosity was involved. It was a game that made chasing the news fun.

Judy was a real pioneer in electronic journalism, improvising in a field where there were few guidelines. She gave full coverage to the news with follow-up stories, something that is seldom done today. Her newscasts were crammed with local news, letting listeners know what was going on in the city.

Her book shows that people who ordinarily refused to talk with the press opened up to her. In her long career in print journalism, electronic media, and public relations, people found it easy to talk to her. Unlike many of her modern-day counterparts, she did not ask stupid or offensive questions. She prepared for interviews by reading and finding out all she could about the subject in advance. As a result, they felt they could talk to her as an equal, for they knew she was knowledgeable and trustworthy.

This book reveals a great deal I did not know about Judy's early life. I always knew that she had deep feelings about the unfortunates that news people are exposed to. She guarded well against the occupational hazard afflicting many veteran reporters who are exposed to blood and guts, criminals, cops, and lawyers—the exposure makes many of them hard and cynical. She remained compassionate and dedicated to the job.

Once, a police lieutenant was telling me we were making far too much of the arrest of a policeman for burglarizing a liquor store. "Just because he was a policeman shouldn't be big news," he said.

Judy overheard. "Listen," she told him, "when the time comes that a policeman caught committing a crime isn't big news, we're in a lot of trouble."

Her early experience on small weekly newspapers gave her a strong sense of community. Doing it all was an advantage later, when she gathered dozens of stories for her broadcasts. Working for a daily newspaper conditioned her to deadline pressure, and sharp editing honed her writing skills, a talent sadly lacking in both local and national telecasts today.

The number of celebrities Judy encountered in her career is

amazing. She brought out facets of their personalities that made them human. One is a touching story of Vail Ennis, sheriff of Bee County, who had a reputation as a bully and killer. She brought out a very different side of his personality.

She dealt with tycoons as easily as with convicts. She never played the new journalism game of "gotcha," with its object of asking trick questions designed to embarrass or bring down a public figure. She never allowed her reporters to show bias, even though they felt strongly about their politics.

When she "retired" to work in the public arena with the Council of Governments, her experience was valuable in mediating disputes between various factions, showing them how mutual cooperation works to their advantage.

To sum up Juliet Knight Wenger, you'd have to say she is a "people person" who knows more about South Texas than anybody else I know. It is a real treat to hear her tell about it.

—Bill Walraven

Landing a Job

Somehow I managed to grow up in Texas believing the Smith Corona to be more powerful than the Smith & Wesson. From the age of nine, I was intent on being a newspaper reporter and changing the shoot-it-out world with a typewriter.

By age twenty-one, I was saying to myself, "Look at me. I'm a successful journalist." I should have been more objective than to make that boast, but in 1939 the country was in a deep depression, and having a job was a success in itself. I had graduated from the School of Journalism at the University of Texas, and the dean, Paul J. Thompson, had done the impossible. Resolutely, he searched until he saw to it that I was employed.

My first job was editor of the *Brazoria County Review*, a weekly paper in Angleton, a small county-seat town south of Houston. Its total assets were a typewriter and a telephone. We printed the paper in the nearby town of Alvin, where the publisher edited a paper for someone else until he got fired.

Finding my way around the town that was my beat was easy. The courthouse, with a jail on top, was the tallest building in the community. There I could find out who was arrested, who had gone on trial, and what county commissioners were doing. That should fill the front page.

Oh, yes, I had a telephone book, which took care of the society column. I just went down the alphabet, calling, asking who had company over the weekend or was going to Houston shopping.

As for advertising, right away I spotted a pharmacy, a movie house, and a combination funeral home and furniture store on the main street. They all needed to promote their businesses. I knew absolutely nothing about selling or laying out advertising, and cared even less, but surely it couldn't be difficult.

I anticipated that by the end of the week, when I got my first paycheck of twenty-five dollars, or perhaps the second week, I should have enough savings to buy a bicycle. This would be my first investment as an independent woman and a capitalist in the work force.

Two state highway patrolmen stationed in Angleton took turns running along the main street, holding my bicycle upright while I learned to balance.

I was cocky when I assumed my editorial position Monday morning. I had not been so Sunday, when I arrived in Angleton from Corpus Christi. When I parted from my father, I held on to him tight. He said, "You don't have to go, you know."

I looked at him in amazement. My parents had made huge sacrifices to put me through college. Self-righteously, I informed my father that from now on, I paid my own way.

He put me on a bus traveling down the Hug-the-Coast Highway. I had never lived in a town as small as Angleton. For some reason, I expected it to be puritanical and mean. Before we pulled into the bus station there, I took a package of cigarettes out of my purse and left them on the seat. I would not smoke, drink, or do anything to bring the wrath of judgmental people down upon my head.

I had arranged in advance to rent a room in a boarding house run by a Mrs. Moulder. For seven dollars a week, I would have a place to sleep and three meals a day. No one was at home when I walked into the house and into my ugly, bare little room. One glance, and all of my illusions of sophistication hung in shreds around what had formerly been composure.

Walking out the front door, I stood on the lawn feeling shipwrecked on a little island of isolation. Then I noticed a moving van slowly making its way down the narrow street. My uncle, Perry C. Tucker, owned Corpus Christi Transfer, a Mayflower affiliate. One

Juliet on bicycle.

of his vans was scheduled to make a delivery to Houston, so he had agreed it could drop off my trunk.

The van stopped, and out stepped Victor. He was one of my uncle's long-time drivers whom I had known throughout my childhood. He must have been astounded when I burst into tears and threw my arms around him. He helped me climb into the cab of the truck and listened while I told him how frightened I was, on my own, in a town where I knew no one.

"Come on," he said. "We'll go have a beer and you'll feel better." He drove the big van across the railroad tracks and parked it at a honky-tonk. Western music was playing on the jukebox.

I began to tell Victor how important it was to me to be an insightful reporter who recognized and made public what needed to be known. I explained to him my beliefs that those in the Fourth Estate had to hold those who control government and business accountable for Texas and these United States to be all that we expected of them.

How wise I thought myself. Yet, what I was repeating to the Mexican-American truck driver with little formal education was what many of us in journalism school at that time considered to be intrinsic truth.

I bought a new package of cigarettes, and we each drank a beer and laughed about how silly I had been to be afraid. The affectations with which I had planned to impress the natives had lasted less than an hour. When Victor left me back at the boarding house with my trunk to unpack, I was resigned to be me, vices and all.

The residents of Angleton turned out to be attractive, well educated, and well traveled, many of them from pioneer Texas families. Angleton lies on the banks of the Brazos River, which winds its way through Texas history from the days of the Republic in the 1840s.

It turned out to be the most egalitarian town I've ever encountered, where the banker's wife and the beautician were in the same bridge club. The pretentious few provided grist for the humor of the many.

I was quickly accepted in the little Episcopal church as a good source of manual labor for polishing altar brass. Lizanet Delaney, daughter of the local pharmacist, and I entertained ourselves while we worked, by checking to see whether the picture of the previous minister was hung face-out or to the wall that day.

One of the altar guild members, an elderly spinster, always turned the picture to the wall, because this minister had been exposed as a homosexual. Others in the congregation turned it back around, saying he was a fine preacher and that his sexual preferences were none of their business. I don't know why they didn't tuck the picture out of sight in a drawer. Guess that would have spoiled the jocundity.

As a reporter, I slipped ebulliently into a routine. My boarding house was only two blocks from the fire station. I slept with a pair of coveralls beside my bed. When the siren sounded in the middle of the night, volunteers ran to the station, backed out the truck, and drove by my house. I would wait for them on the curb, ready to hang onto the back of the truck, covering my big story of the week.

The sheriff's deputies and highway patrolmen let me ride with

Landing a Job 5

them on patrol or investigations. The Texas Ranger didn't let me work cases with him, but he did take me to coffee. That was a real treat, because he "saucered and blowed." I had never before seen anyone pour his coffee into his saucer and drink it from the rim, but the Ranger did it most gracefully. I would have tried it if I had dared, but I feared the strong, hot liquid would run out of the corner of my mouth and down my chin.

It would have been inconceivable to that cub reporter that more than fifty years later a woman would spill hot coffee on herself and, because she was burned, sue the establishment that brewed the coffee. There was a common belief then, at least for people we knew, that court decisions were erudite.

My generation had been taught in both our classrooms and in Sunday school all about the good in people, but we were carefully sheltered from information that might give us clues that there are shades of good and bad. We expected people with whom we associated to tell the truth and to be honorable and equitable.

Covering district-court criminal cases gave me my first inkling that this wasn't true. A white man who killed someone of no special prominence could probably get off with a five-year suspended sentence. A black man who stole a horse or cow might be hanged. This was a shock, but it helped me to sort out and discard myths that I had accepted as unquestionable facts.

The newspaper's publisher told me that the county commissioners were crooked and that I should try to dredge up anything that would prove them to be corrupt. Never doubting my publisher's integrity, I poked around everywhere I could but found nothing relevant.

Soon after that, the commissioners voted to give our newspaper a share of the legals. Legal notices are profitable business. Publishers vie to be the official newspaper of a county, city, or school district. Federal and state laws mandate the publication of long, wordy notifications of certain public hearings or anticipated actions, and they pay well by the word.

When this new revenue started coming in to our paper, the publisher explained to me that he had been misled into thinking the commissioners were less than honest. He now knew them to be men of integrity, and I was to cease trying to prove otherwise. It took me hardly any time at all to figure that one out.

It's a good thing I lost my naiveté before I hired Joe Duhan. He was one of a number of young boys who sold papers for me on the street each week. He was a handsome, dark-haired boy with charisma. His single mother worked as a cashier at the local movie house, so he was free to roam at all hours.

He made friends with me, working me for everything I was worth. He was in and out of trouble, only twelve years old. There were no juvenile officers or shelters then. I didn't want him sent off to what was called a "reformatory," which was never known to reform anybody.

I agreed to be responsible for Joe. Each morning that I took him to the front door of his school, he walked out the back. When I got him into Boy Scouts, he broke into the hut and stole the troop's fund.

Joe nursed me when I had one of my periodic attacks of undulant fever. Normally, I ran a low-grade fever, but with these attacks, the fever shot up and I retained only the most tenuous touch with reality. Even so, lying in my bed, I kept the keys to the company car under my pillow and made sure Joe didn't get them, despite all the tricks he tried.

As delinquent as that juvenile was, he proved to be the best little nurse I ever had. He would steal from me if he got a chance, but he loved me in his way and took care of me with a gentle maturity.

After our time together in Angleton, I don't know what kept him from becoming a criminal. Perhaps some innate good. Years later, he tracked me down and came to see me in Corpus Christi, bringing his wife to meet me. He wanted me to know that he didn't turn out to be a con man. He was a heavy-equipment operator on construction jobs, making a good wage and taking care of his family.

Many people might have considered Angleton, especially in the 1930s, a backwater town. For me, it was an institution of highest learning. People aren't all good. They aren't all bad, either. Angleton wrote in Braille much that had been invisible to my inexperienced eyes.

2
Jailhouse Tête-à-Tête

In Angleton, my news sources included almost anyone in town. As I walked the streets, I often stopped to question public officials or business owners and operators. Small personals reporting the visit of a houseguest or even a resident's shopping trip to Houston made news in a town this size. A lot of my first days working as a reporter were also spent in the offices of the Brazoria County Jail, reading complaints and asking questions, and at the booking desk. I did not go into the cellblocks.

During my first few months in town, deputies arrested a young man on a theft charge. They didn't have much on him, but an instinct that good cops have told them that this was a big catch. In those precomputer days, the process of determining whether a prisoner was wanted anywhere else in the country was a lengthy one.

I was caught up by the acumen of the officers. With little formal education and few technical tools, they could sense what was not apparent to the layman. They read the look in the eyes, the body language, and numerous details that others did not notice. Previously, I had seen an officer get on a bus and point to one man, a wanted man, but a man he had never seen before in life or picture.

This phenomenon made me eager to talk to this prisoner whom

the officers instinctively felt was much more dangerous than a common thief. I asked to be allowed to interview him, and the sheriff agreed. I'm sure they hoped I would learn something that they had not been able to.

The young man was held in a cell far back in the lockup. As the jailer took me there, one cell door, then another, clanged shut after we passed through them. He opened the door of the cell in which the prisoner stood, then locked it behind me.

The prisoner, probably about my age, was handsome and tall, with strong features and an easy, congenial smile. As though he wanted to allay any nervousness I might have, with urbanity he made an effort to put me at ease.

We sat down on a metal bunk and began talking as might two people in a college dorm. He assured me that he was not a thief, that his arrest had been a mistake. I was stunned by the realization that he was extremely well-versed and articulate.

I asked him where he was from. His accent led me to believe he was probably from the East Coast. He told me that he thought of no one place as home, because his family had moved many times. Why had he come to Texas? He had been offered a position in Houston, but it had not materialized.

Never did he appear to be evasive, yet I learned nothing. He questioned me about Texas. He was particularly interested in the environment and geology of the state. A better reporter than I, he learned a good deal more from me than I from him. When the jailer came for me, the prisoner and I shook hands as would two new acquaintances who had enjoyed meeting one another.

The FBI report came in. It confirmed the suspicions of these small-town officers. My pleasant host was a much-wanted serial killer.

He had been under arrest in an eastern state when his father died. Officers agreed to take him to attend the funeral. On the trip, he went into a restroom with police on guard outside the door. He dropped out of a second-story window and escaped. Fugitive charges were filed against him.

This episode taught me a good deal. I was surprised to find out that I was not particularly afraid of criminals, alleged or otherwise. A man or woman could commit monstrous acts without being a monster. Many criminals retain intrinsic characteristics that make them likable, which deepens the tragedy of their deviant behavior.

These realizations gave me warning that as a reporter, I needed to acquire some of the astuteness that the deputies had shown in suspecting this rather charming person.

3
One of God's Strays

What Marguerite McBride taught me, I remember in all seriousness, but when I think of her, I grin.

I met her soon after I arrived in Angleton. We were at some evening affair when I saw her, a short woman with an hourglass figure, wearing a tailored silk dress of muted colors and an insolent little hat.

She walked over to me, a stranger, raised her chin in a comic pose to stare up at me, and then demanded, "How tall are you?"

"Five feet eleven," I replied.

"Do you like being tall?" she asked. "Does it make you feel superior?"

I didn't back off, and I answered her without getting ruffled. "Let's just say I'm more comfortable with it now than I was growing up. It's legitimate. My father is six feet six."

Our eyes locked. She smiled. I did, too. Friends! The first lesson I learned from her in a list of what every reporter should know was to search out people who are not afraid to say what they mean. There aren't many of them. They're enlightening.

Mrs. McBride was a member of a pioneer Texas family and chairman of the board of a local bank. She knew a lot about politics, government, and banking. I thought her paranoid as she described to me how organized crime was gaining a hold in the country, about corruption in government, money laundering, violence.

Mrs. Mc drove a luxury car with a load of dog food in the trunk. Wherever she saw a hungry-looking dog, she stopped and fed it. When a stray wandered up to her house, she opened the gate, and there would be one more mongrel in the large, fenced backyard.

It was not until I was invited to dinner at her home that I received the full impact of the dog population. We ate on a glass-topped table in a sunroom. Under the table was a pack of the stray dogs, looking up at us through the glass, coveting every bite we took.

The table was set with china, crystal, and silver of museum quality. A gourmet meal was placed before us. Ziggie, her housekeeper who served us, had a crushed felt hat on her head and a cigarette hanging out of her mouth.

"Did you read that copy of *Gone with the Wind* that I gave you, Ziggie, and if so, what did you think of it?" Mrs. Mc asked.

"It's heavy. I went to sleep reading. It fell on my face, and I allow it almost smothered me."

"An astute criticism," Mrs. Mc said to her. And to me, "I like Ziggie to read whatever I do. It always gives me a different perspective."

Her husband was a hard-working, successful rice farmer. She called him "Cousin Earl," making fun of herself and other southerners for having so many kissing cousins.

After dinner she told him, "Cousin Earl, Birdie invited me to play bridge tonight. I told her I only play bridge in the daytime. I don't go gallivanting around at night because some other woman might find out how attractive my husband is."

Cousin Earl looked at her with an expression of love deeper than a quiet man could comfortably put into words.

Mrs. Mc loved to shoot darts at anyone she thought to be pompous. Such a man was bank president Oliver Madison, whose clothes were tailored in England. Picking the scroungiest member of a litter of stray puppies, she paraded around town with it, telling everyone she saw that she had named the pup Victoria.

Madison's wife gave birth to a child. The next day, Mrs. Mc was back on the street with the dog, saying in a sanguine voice, "Wasn't it thoughtful of the Madisons to name their daughter Victoria, after my precious puppy?"

Few dared to talk back to Mrs. Mc, as most everybody needed or might need a loan from the bank. The local pharmacist, however, a thrifty man with no foreseeable need to borrow money, stepped out in her path.

"You knew that Victoria was what they were going to name their child, and you named your dog that to make fun of Madison."

Mrs. Mc laughed. "Someone had to take him down a notch."

The pharmacist chuckled affectionately. "Guess it does us all good to be cut down to size every now and then. Never happens to you, does it Marguerite?"

"Fiddlesticks. The good Lord does that to me every day."

She was teaching me that whatever I thought about a human being, I was apt to find out I didn't have an inkling of all there was to know. I overheard a conversation Mrs. Mc had one day with a woman in a faded housedress. The woman was saying, "My Don's excited about going to Houston with you tomorrow to get his glasses fitted. There's not a child in town needs glasses that you don't see that they get them. They ought to write you up in the *Houston Post*, telling people how good you are."

"None of that." Mrs. Mc looked stern. "Remember, getting the glasses is between us. Nothing to be tellin'."

I suspected that Mrs. Mc had a really special relationship with God. Soon after I moved away from Angleton, I heard that Mrs. Mc was ill. She was disoriented, suffering from hardening of the arteries. Today the diagnosis probably would be Alzheimer's.

In my mind, I saw her standing in the window of her bedroom. As though her prayers were reaching me, I could almost hear her words: "They say I'm going to die, God. I worry about Cousin Earl. The widows will start fighting over him at the funeral. Tell you what, God. I'll stop making fun of people and say only nice things about them... if you'll let me live a little longer." In her most coquettish voice, she added, "Is it a deal, God? Amen."

God doesn't have to worry about bank loans, and he doesn't make deals, even for one of his own favorite strays.

Mrs. Mc taught me how newsworthy eccentrics are. Stereotypes are dull to write about. I hear newspaper readers and television viewers today complain about news content. I think that what they are missing are the stories that you find only if you leave the regular beats of government offices and handouts about celebrities.

Those things must be covered, and it takes no work to get those stories. Reporters often don't hear the biggest stories of the day, because they are concentrating on routine assignments. To pick up on "people stories," a reporter has to be intensely interested in everyone he encounters and has to sense the real story, much as a policeman must follow his instincts. People like Mrs. McBride, who always know the pulse of the town, have been for me endless sources of stories that matter.

4
The Iconoclasts

When I began my career as a reporter in Angleton, I would often weigh decisions I had to make by the values my professors taught me in journalism school.

Between the years of 1934 and 1938, when I was a student at the University of Texas, Texas history was getting a thorough going-over from some of the most independent thinkers who had ever gathered in Austin. They were researching, writing, realizing the meaning of the core of Texas being. The most prominent historians and writers were J. Frank Dobie, Roy Bedichek, and Walter Prescott Webb, professors who were never politically correct. They were great friends, each one-of-a-kind, each admiring the others for their powerful stances on freedom and the conservation of this good earth.

Both the Bedicheks and Dobies were friends of my parents when I was a child in Austin. My earliest memory of the Bedichek family is having dinner in their dining room and concentrating on the wall, not the people.

A mural depicting Texas history was painted on a wooden panel that covered one wall and was screwed into it so that it could be moved if the need arose. This huge, vivid oil painting telling a story amazed me. I had not yet seen Mexican murals, with their political themes, so I didn't realize the influences this picture reflected.

My family moved away from Austin. The next memory I have of the Bedichek family is from when I returned to the capital to attend the University of Texas. Roy Bedichek joined Dobie and Webb in leading the liberal cause in support of Homer Price Rainey, president of the University, against what they called "a reactionary board of regents." The liberals lost. Rainey was fired.

Webb, in an essay, spoke for them all. "Men at Oxford are free to follow their compass of truth wherever the needle points without looking over their shoulders to see what hounds are pursuing them... England is not afraid to have views expressed. England, with all its apparent stupidities, seems to know what a university really is."

At about the same time, Arthur Deen, my geology professor, was tried by the Texas legislature for blasphemy. The blasphemy was telling our geology class that at no one time had all the land on this planet been covered by water. Accounting for the great flood described in the Bible, he said that populations could exist only in river valleys. Their world was inundated so far as they knew.

The legislative hearing was a farce. Deen was an articulate, knowledgeable man with the acumen to come to reasonable conclusions, and the more questions the legislators asked, the less they understood the answers. Deen was exonerated.

I was surprised that no one investigated Bill Lee, one of my journalism professors, on grounds that he made students think instead of requiring them to conform to his ideology. Ironically, among the many things he taught me was the danger of making any political predictions.

Pappy O'Daniel, radio announcer, songwriter, and flour salesman, was campaigning with the "Lightcrust Dough Boys," running for governor. Lee told our class, "Remember what I tell you, Pappy can't win. He's making a fool of himself." Pappy won the governor's seat and later defeated Lyndon Johnson to go to the Senate.

Of all the mavericks at the University, J. Frank Dobie was the most fêted in Texas—and across the sea at Cambridge, where he was an exchange professor. He abhorred "the establishment" and held strong convictions concerning the importance of freedom of speech and of the press. He wrote a weekly column that appeared in Sunday papers all over the state.

I had liked and admired Mr. Dobie from the time I was about six years old. As a student at the University, I took two of Dobie's classes, "Creative Writing" and "Life and Literature of the Southwest." Pacing up and down the platform as he lectured, the sturdy, bowlegged man walked as though he had gotten off his horse only moments before. When he came near the end of the platform, totally involved in the tale he was spinning, students drew in a collective breath. Only when he turned without falling off the edge did we exhale.

"When Sam Houston was president of the Texas Republic," Dobie told us during a lecture, "he entertained prestigious French consular officials. Dessert was served at the end of a dinner party. President Houston took a big bite of bread pudding. It was blazing hot. Old rough-and-ready Sam spewed it out all over the formal dinner table. 'You know,' he said, 'many a damn fool woulda swallowed that.'" Dobie roared with laughter, as did we.

We never knew what our lesson for the day might be. Dobie learned that a janitor on the staff could play an accordion. He immediately invited the musician to perform for his class. We danced around our desks to the tune of "Little brown jug do I love thee..."

One of Dobie's pet peeves was a monument to the Alamo built in front of the Alamo itself by the Daughters of the Texas Revolution. "The Alamo *is* a monument," Dobie said. "You can't build a monument to a monument. Anyway, it looks like an incinerator."

That opinion was expressed in his syndicated column, along with a picture of the "detestable" structure. I happened to be in the Dobie home the Sunday morning the Alamo column came out. Dobie spread out on the floor pages from the *Chronicle*, the *Express*, the *Times Herald*, and other Texas dailies in which the column ran. He crawled around from paper to paper, stopped to read a sentence aloud to me, laughed appreciatively, then moved on to the next.

I arrived at his classroom one day with other students, to be told we would receive a walk. Dobie had been arrested; a warrant was served, and he was hauled off to the city jail. He had accumulated and failed to pay a saddlebag full of parking tickets. His exact quote was, "I used to tie my horse to a hitching post here. I'm not going to pay a nickel to park my car on a public street."

The judge assessed a fine against him and ordered him to work it off by typing up arrest sheets. Those of us in his class went as a body to the police station to get our assignment for the next day. He received us with exaggerated graciousness, his blue eyes laughing at such foolishness.

The Iconoclasts 17

Dobie made fun of what he thought to be vainglory. The Library Tower at the University was dedicated while I was in school. It reached up to new heights over Austin. The dedication ceremony was emotional, all of us exuding school spirit and pride. Dobie chided us with the comment, "There's a lot of land in Texas. You don't have to build up to the sky. Lay that thing on its side and put a veranda around it."

Students as well as professors lined up on the sides of either conformity or liberal thinking. Fred Gibson was an outspoken classmate who had returned to college in later years, which was unusual in those days. We worked together on the campus newspaper, and again later on the newspaper in Corpus Christi.

He got by with his nonconformity at the University, but in Corpus Christi, he returned from vacation, dead-broke, to find a pink slip on his desk at the newspaper. However, his friendly, humorous style eventually paid off. His books, such as *Hound Dog Man, Home Place,* and *Old Yeller* were bestsellers and made into movie scripts.

Odds for more spectacular success, as could be expected, were with those who studied the system and played it skillfully. Among these were John Connally, president of the student body, and Cecil Burney, a campus leader closely associated with him. John would go on to become one of Texas' best governors and Cecil became a successful corporate lawyer and a much valued advisor to President Lyndon Johnson.

I wrote a column each week for the *Caller-Times*, reporting on the activities of Corpus Christi students and other campus leaders who were becoming known statewide. When I first knew him, John was dating Ida Nell Brill, University Sweetheart, a Bluebonnet Belle, and a thoroughly likable person. My readers were always interested in news about them. John and Ida Nell would marry, and she would become known to the nation as "Nellie."

Cecil and John were among my best news sources when I was writing the college column. They learned early on how the press could help them achieve recognition in their professional careers.

5
Nothing is Forever

During my twenty-first year, I gained self-confidence, was comfortable in a routine, and felt at home in Angleton. Before the year ended, all this would change.

The turnover began when the publisher of the *Brazoria County Review* was fired from his job as editor of the Alvin paper where we printed each week's issue. He arranged for me to take editorial and advertising copy to a Houston printing plant while he put in place a makeshift plant in Angleton.

With our own shop, I learned to make up pages in type, cast corrections on a Linotype, and handle certain necessities of printing. At about that time, the publisher's brother appeared. He hung around for a few days, after which the publisher called me aside. He told me confidentially that a second publication would be printed there. He and his brother would put out an underground, anti-Semitic newspaper, and I would be expected to write for it.

Horrified, I literally staggered out the door and down the street. I knew nothing at that time of concentration camps in Germany or of people like Anne Frank hidden in attics. We were not yet involved in World War II, and in East Texas it still seemed far away. What I did know was that I would immediately disassociate myself from the *Review* and its publisher.

I gave no thought to where I would go. I was too emotional to think of anything practical.

As I walked, I met Marguerite McBride. She stopped me to say that the bank had foreclosed on a debt owed by the other newspaper in this county-seat town. The bank didn't want the newspaper, but it now owned it. She offered me the job of editor and publisher. I accepted.

This chance encounter fit into a pattern in my life. Whenever I was in dire need, an unexpected solution presented itself. I'm forever amazed when this occurs.

My new domain was a commercial printing plant as well as a newspaper. The office faced the main street, and behind it was a back shop filled with drawers of handset type and a dilapidated Linotype and press. The machinery was held together with such high-tech expedients as string and glue.

There came with the newspaper an extraordinary man, Mack, the printer. He operated the Linotype, made up the pages, set the ads and editorial content, and turned out commercial print jobs. I gave him raw copy. I had no need to edit. He corrected spelling, grammar, and punctuation as he set the type. None of my English teachers could have outdone him.

When I determined what each of us would be paid, within revenues, I figured his worth to be four times mine. There was one required specification in our agreement. After we got the paper out on Thursday night, I would not see him again until Monday morning. He was a long-weekend binger.

Weekends, while Mack was drunk, and on the first two days of the week, I traveled the county. Clute, Sweeny, Freeport, Brazoria, and West Colombia—each little town had its own identity.

Traveling, I was selling ads and gathering news in all the towns, writing when I got back to Angleton at night. Then Mack and I worked without stopping or sleeping on press day, through the night and as much of the following day as necessary. Mack made mechanical repairs as we went along, which required hours, but we never failed to publish.

What news existed was easy to find. In each town there was someone who knew everything that *could* be published in a newspaper—and a lot that couldn't.

In Sweeny, that person was Quillian Garrison's aunt, Louise, whose home was the telephone company. The switchboard, with all its color-coded wires, was in her living room. Quillian was a friend of mine in Angleton.

Aunt Louise went about cleaning her house, cooking, and washing her clothes until she heard the sound of a customer calling. Putting on her headphones, she intoned, "Operator." She usually chatted before she put the call through. Nearly everyone was on a party line. Most of the news I collected the readers would already know from the party line, but they wanted to see it in the paper.

This was an era of intinerant printers. An old man named Pete passed through town and applied for a job. I hired him. In a short time, Mack and I knew that he was a nice fellow, but he could not handle the job. We couldn't afford a nonproductive employee.

I took him to a restaurant and over coffee told him I had to let him go. I hated myself. I liked this man. My words came out in little choking sounds as tears drained from my eyes. Pete consoled me. Before he left town, he brought me a gift, a pair of nylons. Nylons were casualties of the war in Europe, MIAs. Who knows where he found them.

Little of my time could be stolen from work for recreation, but I'd often sneak away at the hour the one train of the day passed through town. One of my romantic streaks is a train track. I loved the sounds of what was then a steam train and the metal wheels rolling on the track.

The train came through at full speed and did not stop unless notified in advance that there was a passenger or cargo to pick up. Orders were handed up to the engineer on a piece of paper attached to a string that formed a triangle at the top of a forked stick. When I was around, the stationmaster allowed me to perform this glorious task. The engineer, reaching out of the locomotive window, ran his arm through the triangle, capturing the string and message.

The days of such simple pleasures were about to end. The disruption of our lives occurred on a Monday. Quillian and I drove to Freeport to see a friend. We had no radio in the car. When we arrived at the friend's house, no one greeted us. Everyone was seated in a circle around a radio as large as today's big-screen televisions.

President Roosevelt's familiar voice was coming from the radio speaker. "Yesterday, December 7, 1941, a day that will live in infamy, the United States was suddenly and deliberately attacked by naval and air forces of the empire of Japan... I regret to inform you that many American lives have been lost."

Instantaneously, I, a lifetime pacifist, was a converted patriot. Silently, I pledged my loyalty to the president. My world expanded beyond Texas borders across oceans in each direction. I wanted to serve my country. I pondered, how could I best do that? An answer came to me. *Learn to fly*. That was something I had always intended to do. I knew that women couldn't go into combat, but I knew that they were being used to fly in troops and cargo.

Again, a way opened up to me that I felt I was intended to take. Paul J. Thompson, the journalism school dean, recommended me to George Atkins. Mr. Atkins, owner and publisher, offered me a job as editor of the *Beeville Bee-Picayune*, then, as now, one of the most respected weeklies in Texas. Not only was it my newspaper of choice, Beeville had an airport and a flight instructor! I was elated at the thought that I could do my job as a reporter in Beeville and at the same time earn my pilot's license. I gave Mrs. Mc my resignation, regretfully leaving behind the *Angleton Times* and Angleton, a small Texas town that proudly lives its history.

6
So This is War

During the first months of World War II, I worked in Beeville for George Atkins at the *Bee-Picayune*. Mr. Atkins was one of the grand old men of Texas journalism. He was the first of several mentors from whom I was fortunate enough to receive on-the-job-training.

I was also part of Beeville's civil defense. My first symbol of participation in the war effort was a key given to me by City Secretary Ellis Quinn. City hall was now also Civil Defense Headquarters. If a bomb attack came, I was to let myself in with the key and take part in protecting the city. We seriously considered such an attack a strong possibility.

The mayor, Doug Hermes, was a shy young man who wanted the city to be well-informed, but he was not articulate and found public speaking torturous. He would give me information, saying, "You put it in words like it should be."

When the first papers ran off the press, Hermes stopped by for his copy. He'd tell me, "I want to know what I said this week before somebody asks me."

Most reporters in that era tried to put words accurately in context so that readers would understand their meaning and get a sense of what the news source wanted to say. Today, the tendency is to wait for a public official to misspeak and then say, "Gotcha."

Hermes' term ended, and Jim Ballard succeeded him. An older man, a rancher and bank president, he was articulate. During my first interview with him, he was sitting in front of the barber shop whittling out a tiny cowboy boot, embossed as though it were made of leather.

Beeville was still rural. There were no dial phones but a live telephone operator. When she said, "Number, please?" I'd say, "I want to talk to Mayor Ballard at the bank."

She'd correct me, "Oh, he's down at the barber shop. I'll ring there."

Primarily, Beeville was a business and social center for ranches, a delightful town to cover. People were starkly individual and friendly. They enjoyed one another. J. Frank Dobie, who grew up in this ranch country, was a friend of Mayor Ballard. These men were comfortable around bonfires with cowhands, exchanging stories of cattle drives and rustlers. Dobie wrote columns that we carried in the paper frequently.

At night, the value of chips piled high on card tables at the Country Club would make a casino dealer in Las Vegas envious. These "small-town" families were not what you'd call "country people." They took off in their private planes to fly to New York for a daughter's debut or to see a son play football with an Ivy League team.

When the sons and daughters came home, formal dances were held at Hotel Kohler. Youths wore tuxedos with cowboy boots. However, they took the tuxes off and donned western shirts and chaps for street dances, swinging out to the "Schottische" and to "Put Your Little Foot." Some nights, we all crowded onto the floor of a dance hall in Skidmore as the jukebox played "String of Pearls" and "Tuxedo Junction."

One by one, the carefree young men slowly disappeared. Some were drafted. Most volunteered. Not many eligible bachelors were left to be dance partners.

For the first time in my working life, I had days off. The *Bee-Picayune* was well-managed and published on time. Jack Hathaway, in the back shop, made sure it produced. He was the only person ever able to read my handwriting. I could take my notes to him and ask, "What did I write here?" and he could tell me.

Weekly papers are almost always devoted to local news. At that time, readers wanted news of what was happening in far-off places to their husbands, sons, and friends. Once in a while, a big story managed to bring our attention back home, but other weeks nothing deserved a top headline unless it related somehow to the war effort.

7
Sweet and Sour Justice

Law-enforcement officers and reporters have certain things in common. One of them is the knowledge that there is little equity under law. The criminal justice system and the judicial system work some of the time. When they don't, it is hard for those close to it to continue to believe in the system.

Vail Ennis was an officer I respected. He was strict in enforcing the law as he read it, dealing fairly with people of any color or income category. He did what he believed to be right.

Vail was sheriff of Bee County when I was writing for the *Bee-Picayune*. We had a good working relationship. He gave me access to breaking news, and I made sure I did not expose information prematurely that would damage the making of a case.

The prototype of a Texas sheriff, lanky, leather-skinned, erect in starched khakis and cowboy hat, Vail cast the long shadow that was the symbol of the western lawman. He was of the old school, stuffing gun powder into shells to make his own bullets. At the same time, he was abreast of development in detection and lab techniques. He stood for integrity to the people of the town.

My most indelible impression of the sheriff was stamped into my mind the day I answered the phone and heard him say, "Come on over to my office. I have a slavery case!"

I ran the short, hot distance to the courthouse from the newspaper. In the sheriff's office, sitting in a straight chair at a small table, was a shrunken black man, his hair a loosely knit scouring pad with bits of sawdust, twig, and leaf embedded in it. He wore what had once been shirt and pants, but by then they were strands of filthy cloth.

He looked my way for a moment, long enough for me to recognize frantic fear like that seen in the eyes of animals caught in traps. Vail stood in the middle of the floor, legs apart, maintaining equilibrium as a skipper stands on the deck of a heeling sailboat.

"I got a tip," the sheriff said. "Went out to the Buena Vista Ranch. Found him in a chicken coop. No chickens. Nothing. Best I can figure out, they gave him some flour most days. He could mix it with water and make a kind of bread. I don't know how many years he's been enslaved. He doesn't know, either."

"Does he have a name?"

"If he has, he's forgotten it. I guess he used to talk. Nobody to talk to so long, he sort of grunts."

The nameless remnant of humanity showed no signs that he heard or understood what was being said.

Vail's voice had an echoing quality, as though he were trying out words, bouncing them back and forth against the walls of his lungs until they found their way out. "I filed a charge of slavery. Don't know when that charge was last filed in this part of the country."

The door opened, and a deputy walked in carrying a bowl, a jar of molasses, and a loaf of store-bought bread.

The frightened pair of eyes focused on the articles in the deputy's hands. The eyes shone, remembering, anticipating, finally believing.

"'Lasses!" It was somewhere between the bleat of a baby goat and a puppy's sharp bark. "'Lasses!" Half rising from his chair, arms shaking, he reached out and made a grab for the jar.

"Take your time," Vail said. "Nobody's going to take the molasses away from you. Sit down."

Slowly, the liberated slave sat. What little vitality remained in his body was spiraled into a tight spring, ready to shoot forward if necessary to seize that dark, sweet liquid.

The deputy set a bowl down on the table in front of him, laid a spoon beside it, and put a piece of bread in the bowl. Then he began pouring molasses over the bread. Before he could finish pouring, the fellow-being sprang. With a low growl, he sank both hands into the molasses and began ladling it into his mouth, ignoring the spoon. Some of the liquid he swallowed, some leaked out of the sides of his mouth. A bit flew into his hair, where it glistened more festively than the other debris.

Tears gushed out of the now-gleaming eyes, surfing down the wrinkles of his face, falling into the bowl to dilute the molasses. Both Vail and the deputy wiped the backs of their hands across their faces to obliterate moisture, as though anyone would have dared to accuse them of crying.

Soon after that, I left Beeville. Over the years, I heard reports that Vail had become a killer lawman, imposing his own form of justice as blatantly as the notorious Judge Roy Bean.

One story, in the *Bee-Picayune*, reported that he had been involved in a brawl while serving papers in a child-custody case. Allegations were that he gunned down three Mexican brothers and kicked the wife of one of them in the stomach.

Later, I heard that Vail had been shot and was not expected to live. I went to Beeville and to the hospital where he lay in bed, the strength sapped from a powerful man. I took his hand and sat beside him, and we talked as we always had, honestly, no cover-ups. I asked him about the reports I had heard.

"You have to understand," he pleaded. "It's not like it used to be. Streets aren't safe any more. Courts won't punish crime. Criminals know they can do whatever they want to and be back on the street next day.

"I was elected to enforce the law. If the courts won't do it, I have to. You know that, don't you? I'm the sheriff. If I don't do the right thing, who will? Who's going to take care of women and children?"

He had eliminated the grand jury and courtroom and moved at full speed from arrest to judgment and punishment. In a way, I understood. I had consoled so many victims of crime. I had felt the frustration of victims forgotten while the criminals used the system to avoid the consequences of their crimes. The odds were stacked against ordinary people playing by the rules.

Vail kept telling me of case after case in which the system had failed. He had to stop often for breath. "People are strong," he said.

"They can handle tragedy and crisis in life, but not time after time if the bad guy never gets what's coming to him."

Holding Vail's hand as tightly as I could, I said, "The world's spinning out of orbit, isn't it? I still have to believe in miracles. Remember, Vail, the time molasses flowed over devastation, sweetening a flawed world?"

8
A Short Flight

Each week, as soon as we put the *Bee-Picayune* to bed, I headed for the airport. Like most of the other student pilots, I was intent on earning a license so that I could go into the service and do my part in the war effort. I joined a flying club that bought blocks of time for five dollars an hour from our instructor, Oscar Travland, a farmer-pilot who had built a runway through a cotton patch. We flew a Taylorcraft owned by Oscar.

Oscar had a herd of cows, and we had to land at milking time. One day, he got out of the plane and said to me, "You are ready to solo." He walked away to the milking shed. As I took off, the wheels of the plane left the ground almost immediately instead of rising slowly after a speed-building run down the landing strip as they had in the past. I came around and landed, telling Oscar something was wrong.

Oscar spoke only when necessary. "You and that plane together didn't weigh anything after you jettisoned my two hundred and twenty-five pounds." That hadn't occurred to me.

Nearly any time I am involved in a different activity or meet a new person, this gives me leads to stories that I would never have thought to write. My flights in those Beeville days seldom failed to give me news leads.

On my first cross-country, I flew into a controlled airport at

Corpus Christi. Young navy pilots were practicing there. They gloried in buzzing my plane when they realized a girl was flying it. I had no radio, but took instruction from red and green lights given me by the control tower, and I landed uneventfully.

My father met me for coffee in the airport. I looked at him and realized his face was pulled to one side as though it were partially paralyzed.

"What's the matter with your face?" I asked him.

"I don't know," he replied. "I was waiting for your mother to notice it and make me go to the doctor." We both laughed and thought no more about it.

By the time I was ready to leave, a high wind had come up. I taxied out to the runway, got a red light, and before the light turned green, a gust of wind blew me off the taxiway. This happened several times. By the time I was lined up with the runway and had a green light, I was frustrated and frightened.

I flew back to Beeville, landed, and ran to Oscar, who was sitting on a milking stool. Expecting accolades, I boasted, "I managed to take off under the most adverse wind conditions and get back safely."

Without taking his eyes off the cow's udders, he spoke in rhythm with the beat that squirts of milk made hitting the bucket. "If I had thought you couldn't do that, I wouldn't have let you take the plane in the first place."

A few days later, I learned that cancer had been found in a gland in my father's throat. Luckily, a job opened up at the *Corpus Christi Caller*, to replace a reporter who had gone to war.

I moved back to my family home, thinking no more of flying military cargo in the war effort, only of what would be an unsuccessful fight for my father's life.

In Corpus Christi, where I covered navy news, among other things, war still dominated our lives. Father followed the war hour after hour on BBC radio every day of the two years that he survived. He almost lived to celebrate the armistice, but not quite.

He had been, during the first years of his life, a proper little English boy. Long curls fell to the shoulders of his Lord Fauntleroy suit when his parents took him to the London Zoo for his seventh birthday. He was standing in front of the monkey cage eating an apple when a monkey reached through the wire of the cage, took the apple from Father's hand and snatched a curl out of his head by

Launcelot Knight.

the roots. As my father stood bleeding, the monkey alternately took a bite of curl and a bite of apple. Father's parents chose, as a gift to make him forget his pain, two tiny Venetian vases, which are on my dresser now.

His oldest brother, Percy, an architect, had come from England to San Antonio on a commission and stayed. My paternal grandparents, Father, and his brother Hugh later came to San Antonio to join him.

San Antonio was a cowtown when he arrived. No one rode to the foxes here. In chaps and sombrero, they rode with their hounds in brush and pastures. With the teasing my father received, he totally changed his identity in a matter of days. His hair was cut short and his clothes became rugged. He claimed to have acquired a Texas accent almost instantaneously.

The only circumstance under which he would speak with an English accent was to entertain me when I was ill. His favorite song, of all things, was "Oh, Susannah": "I come from Alabama with a banjo on my knee...."

Among the gifts he gave me was the confidence to become a reporter at a time when there were few women in the ranks. He took it for granted that I could do anything I wanted to do. So, in my career, it never occurred to me that there was something within reason that I could not do.

Any time I was away from home, Father wrote to me every day, short letters with whatever news he knew, always ending with "I love you."

News of the whole world was important to father. The English, being part of an empire, have always played international news much higher than is common in the United States.

My mother, who was reared on a Kentucky plantation, met my father on the ranch of a mutual friend when she was visiting Texas. But before she married him, she was a society writer on the staff of the *Kansas City Star*, then one of the nation's best newspapers. Accordingly, news was something my parents always emphasized and discussed with me, and newspapers were something I grew up reading, along with *Heidi* and *The Bobbsy Twins*.

9
Law and Disorder

Crimes have certain elements in common, wherever and whenever encountered. They also vary among states and countries and large towns and small. In the same way, law enforcement follows basic patterns but is distinguishable in each place and time.

In small towns, everyone involved knows what's happening because officers and reporters are constantly exchanging information on an informal basis. The larger the community, the more complex the structure, and the greater the need for defined lines of communication.

Working first in two small towns, I was accustomed to getting most of my stories firsthand at the same time officers made their arrests or investigations. When I started reporting for the *Caller* in Corpus Christi, I encountered all sorts of difficulties. What I didn't realize at first was that this community, until then a small town, was feeling its way toward bigness. If any system was in place, it was one of confusion.

During my first days of reporting there, the only officer I knew on a personal basis was George Denton, FBI agent in charge of the Corpus Christi area and a friend of my father. I went to George with my frustrations.

He was in his office in the federal building. A man I hardly noticed was looking at files in another part of the room. I told George what a terrible time I had getting accurate information from the local police department. "The entire operation is sloppy," I told him. "Complaints are not on file and accessible. Detectives put official reports in their pockets when they go out to work cases. Public records are in disorder."

George commiserated. "I have to work with them. Really makes it tough."

Encouraged, I laid it on heavier. "Total lack of coordination. This isn't a team, it's a gang of single shooters!"

George boomed, "Yeah, it's hell!"

I happened to catch a glimpse of the face of the man across the room. His eyes were brimming with laughter. I looked back at George, and he was convulsing.

"What's going on here?" I demanded.

"I forgot to introduce you," George said. "This is Tommy Matthews, one of Corpus Christi's hopelessly incompetent detectives."

Feeling the fool that I was, I stood mute while the two men had their fun. Tommy was a slender, medium-tall man with a jaunty walk. The brim of his hat was pulled over one of his expressive eyes at an impertinent angle.

He approached me, and his hilarity changed to empathy. "In a way, you are right. We are a small force, growing now, but each still operating in his own way. We file most of the details in our heads, but we do communicate. Each of us knows what the other is doing. Come by my office in the mornings. I'll see to it you get what you need in time to make your deadlines."

Within a short period of time, Tommy had me oriented, and he also encouraged the other officers to cooperate with me. He taught me more about police work than I could have learned in a college-level criminal justice course, if there had been such a thing then.

He preferred to be gentle and considerate but could be hard as diamonds if he had to be. One of the first things he told me was that an officer never shot to deter or wound. If it was a life-threatening situation, he shot to kill. Tommy never did shoot a person.

When I walked into a restaurant or some other public place with him, he did not appear to scrutinize people. Yet, if you quizzed him, he could give you information about every person in the room. I asked him how he did this.

His answer was, "If enough people you have arrested or testified against have promised they'll kill you, you'll learn how to take a quick snapshot of an entire setting within your vision and sit with your back to the wall."

He arranged for me to take the course that was given to rookie cops, including marksmanship taught by an FBI agent.

I learned to shoot well enough drawing from the hip but was never able to make good scores aiming at a target. Finally, Tom and the agent told me, "Take your gun home, clean it, and put it away. Anybody who knows anything about guns would take one look at you, sense that you are not going to pull the trigger, take the gun away, and kill you with it."

I did as they suggested. That gun was the only one I kept from my father's gun collection. Later, after my father died, Tommy sold all the rest of Father's firearms for me. By that time, Tommy was chief of detectives and had pulled together a capable and accountable force.

When I was working on the night shift at the *Caller*, I rode with patrolmen or traffic officers after deadline. It is difficult for this to happen today. Court rulings in numerous cases have distanced reporters from law-enforcement officers to protect the civil rights of suspects and convicted criminals. This makes it hard to establish the trusting relationships that we knew.

Today, crimes are so prevalent that calls are backlogged for officers to answer. In that day, we'd go long periods of time with no calls. I liked to ride with Watson, who worked sometimes as a patrolman and sometimes as dispatcher. He took along his guitar, and when we had nothing else to do we would meet with other cars and have a sing-along.

What scared me more than anything were chases. I was in the back seat of a patrol car one night, with a veteran officer in the front passenger seat and a young officer driving. The driver saw a car in motion without headlights burning. Thinking it was an oversight on the part of a civilian driver, the policeman touched his siren to get his attention. The car with no lights took off at a high speed. We were in pursuit.

We drove all the way across town and finally onto a country

road at speeds sometimes exceeding one hundred miles an hour. The driver of the lead car kept opening the door as though he were going to jump out. We were right on his tail. The veteran officer was screaming at our driver, "Fall back. We'll all get killed if he jumps and we hit that car." The wise voice was ignored.

The pursued, who by now we felt sure was in a stolen car, lost control of his vehicle. The car came to a halt suddenly, automatically slamming the door open and ejecting the driver. He was thrown into the brush and took out on foot.

The two officers jumped out of the patrol car to give chase. The older officer told me to call the dispatcher for backup, and both officers disappeared from sight.

The left front window of the patrol car was broken out, so I couldn't lock the door. I grabbed a spotlight and held it, ready to hit the stolen-car driver if he doubled back and tried to steal the patrol car.

I radioed in. Watson was dispatching. My voice was shaking as I told him where we were. He put the location out on the air, then came back on the radio with me, giving me encouragement.

It was black out there, with no moon, far from city lights. With Watson's voice as a suit of armor to shield me, I sat shaking, holding my spotlight. Within a short period of time, headlights began appearing from every direction. It could have been the choreographed opening of the Olympic games as a marathon of torchbearers converged on me.

There were city police, state troopers, sheriff's deputies, fire cars, and any other emergency vehicle within the reach of my terrified voice. The car thief got away, but I shook all night in my bed. I can still visualize that chase and begin to tremble.

So many times, I held injured people in my arms at wreck scenes. During the war, the police forces were as short of men as newspapers were. Since I was riding with them anyhow, patrolmen trained me to help at crime or wreck scenes. I learned to take measurements, gather evidence, and assist the injured. This is something that insurance costs have since made prohibitive.

As long as I was involved in helping, I was unemotional, however terrible the injuries or the cries of the injured. When our work was done, though, I sometimes fainted. Police would throw me in the back seat of the car and open the windows, and by the time we got back to the station I'd be in good shape.

I had lived with undulant fever since I was five years old, but it was not yet diagnosed. When the fever was high, I might lose consciousness without any advance notice. I did so while taking pictures at one wreck and fell on broken glass, receiving minor cuts. Ambulance attendants picked me up on a gurney, thinking I was a wreck victim. I regained enough strength to explain the situation to them before they hauled me off.

Even crime, it seemed, was rationed during the war. World War II gave us a community of interest that encouraged us to be more considerate of one another as a means of survival. Crimes of passion—stabbings in bars, and murders—continued, but there were fewer crimes of economic greed, such as robberies and burglaries.

Even the vice squad had an easy time of it. A red-light district on Sam Rankin Street clustered prostitutes in one area. Those who defied the system and were picked up on the street were known as "Lupe's debutantes." Each morning, Lupe, the police matron, led them into municipal court like a line of schoolchildren. Police officers hailed each by name and made titillating comments.

These policemen were largely self-educated. They knew their trade. For the most part, they recognized the criminals and their methods of operation. When they went to a crime scene, they usually had a good idea of who was involved. Not many criminals were transients or sophisticated con men; most were locals with low mentality or an addiction to bootleg whiskey.

Some officers forgot that they carried guns for protection only. They made mistakes, and sometimes they abused those on whom society set little value—the poor, the powerless. Many more did their jobs conscientiously, showing courage and kindness rather than incivility or oppression. This, I believe, is still true in South Texas.

10
On the Night Side

During the last two years of my father's life, 1944–45, I lived in my parents' home. Father continued to work in his wholesale paper company until a few weeks before his death. We talked not at all of illness and death, but of newspapering and war.

Working for a newspaper during the war made opportunities available to me that would have demanded years of experience in peacetime. I was thrown onto beats to which a new reporter would not be assigned under normal conditions: police, city hall, courthouse, and the federal building.

The *Caller* and the *Times* were owned by the same company and were put out with the same facilities in the same building.

Since there was no radio, television, or other competition at that time, the *Caller* and the *Times* reporters competed against one another. It added a bit of a challenge. The afternoon paper later disappeared, and the *Caller-Times* became a morning paper, as happened in so many cities of the nation.

We lived news and its reporting. I was the first woman to be put on the night-side shift. I went to work at 1:00 in the afternoon and worked until 1:00 in the morning. My deadline for assigned stories was 10:00 P.M., but I was responsible for any breaking news between 10:00 P.M. and 1:00 A.M. Usually, I rode police cars those last three hours.

My city editor was Henry Moore. A short, robust man, he wielded a black marker as cruelly as an Italian bandit would brandish a stiletto. I never made the same mistake twice in writing copy for Henry. His marker underlined my stupidity indelibly. Newspaper copy that Henry sent to the printer was almost error-free.

He was teaching me a great deal every night, the hard way; then he was drafted. That made him mad. He had tried to enlist, but the army had turned him down for having flat feet.

He was ordered to board a train in Corpus Christi. I agreed to drive him to the station. He did not appear at the appointed hour. I began searching the bars. When I found him, he could walk only with difficulty. I rushed him to the station. Too late. The train had left.

I knew the train switched at Odem, about ten miles away. That might give me enough time to catch up with it. Henry slept peacefully beside me while I drove as fast as I dared. We made it.

The train was almost ready to pull out of the Odem station. An accommodating sergeant leaned from the door of the vestibule, reaching out his hand to pull Henry aboard. Henry blasted him drunkenly, "I don't need any help, you son of a bitch!" and heaved himself up into the car at the moment the train jerked and moved forward. I smiled sweetly at the nice sergeant and said, "He's all yours... thank goodness."

In the war years, the navy brought many celebrities to Corpus Christi. Usually, they were available for interviews and were relaxed and friendly with reporters. Among them was the popular movie star Tyrone Power, who was a naval aviator in training. He and his wife, Annabella, a star in her own right, stayed at the Driscoll Hotel.

Annabella, during an interview, told me that she would play the role of a woman prisoner in her next movie. As we talked, she asked about my work and learned that I covered the police and court trials. She asked whether she could accompany me sometime to learn more about the criminal justice system firsthand. I liked her and enjoyed her company, and she made quite a stir wherever we went.

As we were walking to the courthouse one day, we passed an apartment. I pointed it out to Annabella, and we stood for a time looking up as we talked. I explained to her that most police knew who the criminals were and the way each operated. Living temporarily in the apartment to which I was pointing was a man named

Juliet with Annabella Power.

Winters. He was from San Antonio, where he was known as a habitual criminal, a thief and burglar.

He had been shot and came to Corpus Christi to recuperate; he called it "a little R and R." He assured local police that he would not carry out his trade while here. To make expenses, he bootlegged whiskey after-hours. My chief-of-detectives friend, Tommy Matthews, had known Winters for a long time. Tommy took me to Winters' apartment one night to buy a bottle of whiskey.

Winters showed me his scrapbook. In it was pasted every newspaper story about his crimes. He was as proud of it as any Rotary Club president would be of stories of his accomplishments.

When I was walking with Annabella, the wary bootlegger was looking out the window and saw me pointing to the place where he was holed up. In a panic, he called Tommy, fearing that I was betraying him to authorities. Tommy soothed his nerves.

Soon after that, Tyrone was driving out to the Corpus Christi Naval Air Station when he saw a blaze under the porch of a house. Ditching his car, he ran to the house, alerted those inside to escape, and put the fire out himself with a garden hose. A spurned lover had set fire to the building to get even with his "wouldn't-be" girlfriend. Tyrone was as handsome in real life as in movies. His picture as a firefighting hero, shot with my trusted Speed Graphic, rated the front page of the *Caller*.

The hotel in which Tyrone and Annabella were staying was the center of one of our few homefront wartime scares. Submarines had been sighted in the Gulf off Port Aransas, eighteen miles away from the Corpus Christi waterfront. We were under tight blackout restrictions. A call came to police that code signals were being telegraphed by a flashing light from a window in the Driscoll Hotel, probably to German subs.

We converged on the hotel and surrounded it, police, FBI, and navy Intelligence. I would have had a great by-line story, except that what we found was not a spy operation, but a torn blackout curtain swinging in the wind and a florescent light.

The only other major wartime scare was Bill Barnard's story that construction on the bayfront was actually of a Maginot Line like that in France. Fill land on Corpus Christi's shoreline was being created to form T-heads and L-heads into a yacht basin. Bill's story said this was a coverup. He wrote that there was actually clandestine construction of an underground fortress from which troops could fight off the enemy expected to come by sea.

Papers hit the streets with Bill's story, and the town went bonkers. Phone calls came faster than the police, the navy, and the newspaper switchboard operators could answer them. Callers were too frightened to pick up the clue, "Look at the dateline. It's April Fools' Day."

Bill Barnard, one of the best writers the paper ever had, was fired. He went to work for the Associated Press. The next time I saw him, he was vice-president of the Associated Press in New York and took me to lunch in a restaurant high up in Rockefeller Center. The inside joke in the newsroom was that if you wanted to go far in the newspaper business, get fired by the *Caller-Times*. Almost everyone who was fired went to the top. I either didn't stay around long enough, or I wasn't good enough to get fired.

At times, prisoners of war would be brought into Corpus Christi in transit to camps in other parts of the United States. They were held overnight in cells on the top floor of the federal building under custody of the U.S. marshal. German officers nearly always spoke English, so I could interview them. Apparently, journalists in Germany were held in some esteem, as the prisoners treated me politely but were extremely rude to jailers and law-enforcement officers.

In another part of the federal building was the provost marshal's office. The marshal was a captain, all army. In this navy town, he would remind me from time to time, "The marines aren't rugged!" A hearty man, his voice boomed out as though he were addressing the troops. Actually, he had no troops. His was a one-man office.

When I walked in one afternoon, he greeted me with his uproarious laugh. "Look at this," he said, handing me a bill of lading. The powers-that-be had sent him a railroad car full of butter for his troops. Butter was one of those rationed items so rare that few civilians remembered how it tasted. I wrote a short humor story about butter and a possible meltdown. The paper used it as a brightener.

Someone, somewhere, who had goofed, did not think the story was funny. The captain was advised he would be court-martialed for disclosing matters of national security to the press. This called for a little creative writing. I penned a formal letter to the captain, apologizing for having read a bill of lading on his desk and writing a story about it without requesting his permission.

The court-martial was called off, and the captain received a mild reprimand for having insufficient security in his office. I could not make myself feel guilty that I had breached national security in the "butter crisis."

The carload of butter, which had been on a sidetrack at the Southern Pacific yard, went elsewhere.

Around that time, I began investigating cameras. Something new had been developed in Germany, the thirty-five millimeter. No weight to speak of, and it fit in your purse.

Since we were at war with Germany, Leica cameras, which were the best, could not be bought in the United States. FBI Agent George Denton acquired one for me. I didn't ask how. It may have been confiscated from some German prisoner. From then on, photography became a pleasure instead of a task.

I used my Leica to shoot a portrait of a controversial employee, the first city manager. This was a transition period, when the city-manager form of government was being introduced across the nation.

Those accustomed to receiving small favors from city commissioners in their wards were disgruntled when a city manager was named. It made it harder for special interests to operate. Some called this change a fascist move by Germany to destroy democracy. Others said city managers were communists sent to infiltrate local government by Russia. In all my years in city halls, I never found any secret that a foreign power would think worth the cost of planting a spy.

The saddest of days came when President Roosevelt died in 1945. We quickly put out an "Extra," a special edition that electronic journalism later made obsolete. I rushed the "Extra" over to city hall.

We were all benumbed and sat around the council room talking. Some of us had little memory of any other president. Some admired Roosevelt; some hated him. All of us in the city offices that day felt a dread of this upheaval during a war. All agreed that the late president was monumental and had tilted the world scene toward dominance by the United States.

I was in city hall when word came that the war had ended. The building emptied into the streets, as did all others around us. Everyone was shouting and singing, hugging one another. Tommy Matthews came down from the police station on city hall's top floor. He was carrying a high-powered rifle, which he began shooting into the air. Bullets were whizzing by in all directions. No one objected. The joy of long-awaited peace exploded. For a moment in time, everybody in the city, regardless of class or race, loved one another.

11
Old Ways and New

When World War II finally ended, we had difficulty remembering what peacetime living was all about. We didn't go back to where we had been before the war. At first timidly, then with passion, we began to build a new world.

Changes were endemic. Nowhere were they more noticeable than in law enforcement. Nueces County Sheriff John Harney is the name that comes to mind when I think of early-day lawmen. Corpus Christi City Police Chief Earl Dunn represents to me the modernization of the system.

Sheriff Harney fell into one my favorite categories, the honest crook. At times, he might have been testing the law more than enforcing it, but I could always count on what he said, knowing him well enough to recognize his own unusual way of looking at life.

The sheriff was something of a bully. He liked to fight. I'm told—and this was before I knew him—that he used to get mad at men at dances. Harney loomed large. He would, as the story goes, persuade a small, weak friend to get in an argument with the man who had annoyed Harney on the dance floor and invite the man outside to fight. When the man came, ready to beat up on a weakling, he found Harney waiting and took the beating himself.

Harney was one among many officers who drank heavily at

times and enjoyed what nightlife the county had to offer. On one occasion, a city traffic policeman called me at home at 2:00 in the morning. Speaking into the phone in a low voice, he said, "Check the blotter when you get to the police station in the morning. I arrested Sheriff Harney for DWI and leaving the scene." The officer hung up before I could ask more questions, obviously using a telephone on which he was afraid he would be overheard.

I walked straight to the dispatcher's desk when I arrived at the station and checked the blotter. Harney's name was not on it. It was evident that one page had been removed. I asked the sergeant in charge whether Harney had been arrested that morning. He told me no, he had not. I went to the chief, Roy Lay, and got the same answer.

Back at the news bureau, I called Sheriff Harney. I asked him whether he had been arrested. He said, "Hell yes, but I wasn't drunk. I'd only had ten or eleven highballs. I was out working a cattle rustling case, and I was sleepy and tired. I flat didn't see that red light or that car."

I hung out with Harney at the courthouse the afternoon the grand jury was considering his case, teasing him a lot about how long it had been since he or anybody else around here had worked a cattle-rustling case. We got word that the grand jury had reported. A few more minutes and a deputy yelled, "They no-billed you!" I didn't go to the celebration in the sheriff's office that night, not taking any chance on getting picked up for DWI on my way home.

Earl Dunn, on the other hand, moved into the office of chief of police wearing shoes instead of cowboy boots, and no big-brimmed hat. If he carried a gun, it was not conspicuous, because I never saw one.

He delegated authority and let his supervisors know what he expected. They knew exactly how he wanted them to deal with the public, both those involved in crime and their victims. He turned his full attention to his world of equipment and technical capabilities.

Until then, patrolmen drove their beats, stopping at restaurants or other businesses to call in to the station to learn of crimes or disasters, however belatedly. One of the first things Earl did was put radios in patrol cars.

As soon as he had set up a transmitting network and dispatchers were communicating with police cars, he began work on a laboratory. Detectives and lab specialists were trained to examine evidence that would provide forensic testimony for their cases.

Old Ways and New   47

Those things had happened before I began covering the police station for the *Caller*. Earl was installing a photo lab when I started on the police beat. While he was training policemen, he trained me, teaching me to roll bulk film to load my camera and other photographic skills.

Earl was never frivolous, nor was he political. He had such high expectations of people that somehow they lived up to them. It would not occur to him that a mayor, councilman, or person of wealth would seek special dispensations. That made it difficult for them to do so.

Earl was almost too good to be true. He didn't go on the defensive, but learned from well-founded criticism. He accepted others as they were, not as he wished them to be. Creative, he found innovative ways to apply new ideas, devices, or processes, keeping us all up-to-date.

In the years after the war, his radio system needed upgrading. Industry was reconverting to civilian products, but consumerism was explosive, so nearly everything was in short supply. Earl could not find radios to buy in the United States. He tracked down some in Mexico and flew down to pick them up and return them to this country, where they had been made.

When he got back, he complained to me about how miserable the days had been when he was delayed by weather in Mexico City. He didn't leave his hotel room, because he didn't know what there was to do in a foreign country.

I could have fun kidding John Harney. Earl Dunn took me seriously. "That is unforgivable," I told him. "All those wasted days and nights in Mexico, where the dance bands play until daylight. This is the first thing for which I have ever faulted you."

Earl looked at me as though I had misplaced whatever intelligence he had found in me previously.

I kept on needling him. "Oh, well, I guess it is a good thing you didn't know about all that. You would have called the vice squad."

For the only time in his life, he spoke to me indignantly. "I would have done no such thing. I was outside of my jurisdiction."

12

McCracken and Mulvany

Peopled with talented, but somewhat unorthodox characters, my years on the *Caller-Times* were unforgettable.

The luminaries were Bob McCracken and Tom Mulvany. Bob was the editor of the paper and wrote a front-page column called "The Crow's Nest." Mulvany was the erudite reporter.

When Bob graduated from college in the early days of the Depression, he was unable to find a job. He moved into a tent on Padre Island and lived as a beachcomber until a job opened up. In a way, he was solitary, but he became one of the most popular and sought-after civic leaders in Corpus Christi. Shyness made his crowded existence painful, but he could not refuse to participate whenever it was expected of him.

As a teenager, I read his column daily. Occasionally, I stood in front of the plate glass window of the newspaper office, on Mesquite Street at that time, and watched him at work. He was everything I admired. When I went to work on the *Caller*, he became my boss. I found in him common sense, objectivity, and the kindest humor.

MEN... SATURDAY IS BOB McCRACKEN DAY!

you'll be a cool character, too, in these SPORT SHIRTS

Take off your ties... take off your coats. Get out of your warm suits. It's time to relax. Now you can be cool and comfortable in sport clothes.

Bob McCracken.

"Laid-back" was not yet in the English vocabulary, but that's what McCracken was. Among the columns he wrote were those urging men living in this semitropical climate to revolt, to discard their business suits and wear something new in male fashion, the sport shirt.

Bob had a Clark Gable masculinity and the kind of vulnerability that women could not resist; they pursued him. One of the assignments that I grew into on the news staff was to be his shield. When a woman asked him to drive her home from some event, he could not be so impolite as to refuse. Instead, he gave me a signal, and I rudely shouldered my way into his car and sat between him and the woman in the front seat. Some of those women probably dislike me to this day.

On doctor's orders, McCracken quit smoking. Unfortunately, he wrote himself into a corner with a self-righteous column about how much guts it took to quit. Then he started smoking again. When no one was looking, he would light a cigarette and hand it to me. Whenever he passed by my desk, he would take a drag from it. Often, there were two cigarettes going at once in my ashtray. At a young age, he would die of emphysema.

Bob was not an alcoholic, although he drank too much, as nearly all of us did. A time or two, he was picked up for DWI. In that era, public and police both had the attitude "You shouldn't drive when you are drunk, but [shrug] we are all human." Cops liked McCracken as much as did everyone else in town. Whichever patrolman took him to the station would put him in an outer office and call me. I'd go drive him home.

After his death, a number of us who were McCracken's admirers circulated a petition requesting authorities to name the new high bridge across the ship channel "The Crow's Nest." Other citizens wanted the bridge named for Richard King, member of the King Ranch family, banker and port commissioner. Nobody won. The structure was named "Harbor Bridge" and is usually referred to only as the "high bridge."

Tom Mulvany was as different from McCracken as a member of the same species could be. Tom was an intellectual, a classical musician, and a drunk. He had been a violinist in a symphony orchestra in New York, but his hands were injured in an accident, ending his musical career. He turned to writing and drinking. In

Texas, he considered himself to be exiled with peasants still ignorant of civilization. When I, a woman, was assigned to the night side, he was disgusted. He did not speak to me or acknowledge that I existed.

On the night side, Mulvany and I were thrown together frequently. The *Caller* news staff got off work at 1:00 in the morning. And we followed a routine. We had a few beers together to discuss affairs of the world and our individual responsibilities to bring nations out of chaos.

We laid odds on the possibilities. What would happen next? Each of us put up arguments to support his or her opinion of what should be done at this critical moment in history. One particular night, Mulvany, our resident cynic, began reciting the *Rubáiyàt*:

'How sweet is mortal Sovereignty!'—think some:
Others—'How blest the Paradise to come!'

Mulvany hesitated. One beer too many. He couldn't remember. I finished the verse for him:

Ah, take the Cash in hand and waive the Rest;
O, the brave Music of a *distant* drum!

Mulvany looked across the table and saw me for the first time. If I had read the *Rubáiyàt*, I was bound to be a little above subhuman. We walked out together, arms around each other.

Once I had survived probation and been accepted by Mulvany as being probably no worse than any of my peers, I often typed stories for him when he could not deal with a typewriter. Whatever his condition, the words he dictated were well-chosen and mingled on the page as a form of prose that was sometimes almost free verse.

One afternoon, he was late for work. He finally came in, disheveled, and walked straight over to me. He was a handsome man, with black curly hair, deep blue eyes, and strong features. He spoke in a near whisper. "Do you know where I was last night?"

I told him I did not.

"I don't know, either, or how I got there. I woke up this morning in a hotel room in Beeville, in a bed, *alone*! I had to take a taxi back to Corpus Christi."

Blackouts were not unusual for Mulvany. I drove him home one night and helped him into the house. He opened a closet door and showed me shelves of manuscripts. He had written enough short stories to fill a library but had never submitted one to an editor.

He grabbed a fifth of Southern Comfort, lay down on a couch, and was soon asleep. Sitting on the floor in front of the closet, I read manuscripts until daybreak. I selected one, a western story that was exquisitely crafted. At the office that day, I showed it to a *Times* staff writer, Kay Bynum.

Kay belonged to the Byliners, a local writers' club, and submitted Tom's story in a statewide competition. It won first place. Tom was furious at both of us. The next time I saw the story, it was in the Spanish-language edition of *Reader's Digest* and I was in South America. I don't think any of Mulvany's other stories were ever submitted anywhere. He eventually moved to a newspaper in Houston, where he died.

McCracken and Mulvany will be forever linked in the annals of the United States Supreme Court. They were involved in litigation that made journalistic history. It began when I was still working on the *Caller*.

The Nueces County judge was as heavy a drinker as was Mulvany. The judge was a member of a prestigious family. I had known him for some time. Corpus Christi had a polo field and team when I was in my teens. I rode regularly at that time, exercising a polo pony named Sandy.

All the teenagers at the games saw the judge, one of the stars of the team, slip into the harness room from time to time to take swigs from a bottle. We would move the bottle to a different spot where he couldn't find it so he would stay sober and help our team win.

So, it was no surprise to me when he fell off the bench one day while presiding over a case underway at the courthouse. Mulvany was in the courtroom, covering the trial, and reported it as it was.

Texas law does not require a county judge to be sober or hold a law degree. Today most judicial work, except in the smallest of counties, is handled in county court by a county judge-at-law, and the county judge has only administrative responsibilities. At that time, there was no such division of duties.

McCracken wrote in "The Crow's Nest" reasons why he

believed state law should require a county judge to be an attorney who had passed the bar. The column made no inflammatory references to the county judge, but the judge himself thought such were implied.

The judge found both Mulvany and McCracken to be in contempt of court for what they had written and ordered them jailed. The order was carried out. The day the deputies hauled them off from the *Caller-Times*, I walked into the New England Cafeteria for lunch. I heard my name shouted out. It was McCracken's son, Dick, who was hailing me down.

"Juliet, did you know Daddy's in jail?"

Everybody in the cafeteria laughed. The whole town knew.

The Rotary Club, of which McCracken was an active member, had a huge cake with a large saw in it baked and delivered it to his cell. With the sheriff's largess, we all paid McCracken and Mulvany visits behind bars and ate cake.

The two were released on bond, and the case made its way slowly on appeals to the Supreme Court, which finally vindicated both men.

13
Rob's World

During the last weeks of my father's life, a good friend, Harry Garrett, rebuilt his fishing boat, working beside Father's bedroom window so that he could supervise and enjoy his last days. My mother slept few hours in those weeks, and finally became ill herself. After Father died, Mother needed a change, and we decided to leave Corpus Christi. When I gave my resignation from the *Caller-Times* to Bob McCracken it was with deep sadness, but I felt I had no choice.

    A friend of our family, Jack Blackwell, owned a weekly newspaper, the *Rockport Pilot*, and invited me to come to work there to give Mother a new setting. At that time, Rockport was primarily a fishing village, with a boat-building yard on its bayfront that gave the town its identity in the war years.

    Rob Roy Rice, owner of the yard, had stopped building fishing trawlers to build subchasers and landing craft needed in the South Pacific theater. Rob avoided personal publicity, but when he liked a reporter, he would help him or her to get some of the great stories.

    I had no experience covering industry and was not aware of how unusual Rob was among industry executives. Covering government offices is an easy job. The newsmakers have to give you information, and public records are open to you. Industrial CEOs don't have to talk to reporters or divulge information if they don't want to. Most are unavailable to reporters and make what they want to reveal known through public relations experts.

Rob was a big, hearty man, convivial and sure of himself. He had sailed before the mast out of his hometown of Apalachicola, Florida, as a boy on cargo vessels in the schooner trade. Even in the later years of his life, he still had muscles taut as windblown rigging and the agility to take down the main and raise the storm sails in the heaviest blow.

As a young man, he had come to Aransas Pass and built the original shrimp cannery, making this sea delicacy available for the first time to diners inland. Later came freeze plants.

Rob reared a family, sold the cannery, and built the shipyard in Rockport. He had a boathouse constructed on the shore within the shipyard. His crews built the house as they would have a boat, using wooden fasteners instead of screws or nails. The boathouse became the social center of the region. The Capital Press from Austin found it a lazy spot where they could mingle casually with important people from throughout the state.

Rob used these occasions to introduce me to news sources to whom I might not have access otherwise. Such a weekend gave me the chance to get to know Governor Coke Stevenson, which would be helpful to me as long as he was in office. Usually a rather reserved man, the governor would take off his tie, open his collar, and lounge around the bar in the boathouse, talkative. Everything was off the record. Although I couldn't quote him, he provided me with good leads and background information.

The boathouse consisted of a large entertainment area that opened into the kitchen and dining room, and a string of bedrooms arranged so that you walked through one to get to the next. Fairly early in the morning when a party was still lively, Governor Stevenson would announce that he was going to bed. Always polite, he said with his Southern mannerisms, "I warn the gentle ladies who might be coming through my room that I sleep nude." As far as I know, we all respected his privacy.

Tied up under the boathouse was *Rusty*, a forty-three-foot cabin boat also built in the shipyard. Rob laughed at anyone who referred to this as anything other than a "boat." He made fun of "newly rich sailors who call their boats 'yachts' and wear gold braid on their 'yachting' caps."

One of our favorite ways to spend an afternoon was anchoring *Rusty* off an oyster reef, putting on gloves, and collecting oysters. Rob was no slouch at opening them, and they had their full flavor those first few minutes out of the saltwater.

Winnie was always aboard. An exquisite brunette with a model's figure, she had a subtle humor that played right into Rob's sense of fun. He and Winnie were married after both obtained divorces.

Often Rob would invite me to go on the boat when someone that he knew was going to make news would be aboard, thus giving me the first chance at a good story. One night, some visiting oilmen were aboard *Rusty* with us. I informed Rob that John Young, the Nueces County attorney, had told me that he had shut down gambling in Port Aransas. "I don't believe it. Let's go see," Rob said.

The Mustang Island town of Port Aransas was like Galveston, with small casinos behind locked doors. We tied up *Rusty* at Wilson's dock and went into the restaurant for a seafood dinner. After dinner, Rob led us down a hall. He gave a password, and a locked door opened.

A free drink was handed to each of us who walked through the door. One of the oilmen gave me several hundred-dollar bills. I walked over to a craps table and lost those bills before I had time to find out whether I was having fun.

The news story made only a slight stir. Obviously, juggling the truth about a little illegal gambling caused no wave of indignation in the public, as Young was next elected county judge, then sent to Congress.

Rob was not judgmental. He knew how politics worked. He himself asked nothing of any man and gave nothing for which he expected something in return. Both he and Winnie lived by their own criteria, true to what they believed but uninterested in what others thought of them.

Rob sold the shipyard and had the hull of the boathouse moved onto a large lot in an exaltation of ancient oak trees. A picture window that had looked out over Aransas Bay then provided a view of twisting limbs and designer leaves, and beyond that was Winnie's carefully tended garden of old-fashioned roses.

Good news stories were to be found here, too. Winnie was a nationally respected authority on seashells and gave me material that was valuable to beachcombers who lived along the coast.

Her closest friend, Connie Hagar, was the bird woman who attracted the Audubon Society to Rockport and made Rockport a major destination for birders. Connie was gracious and generous with her time in giving me stories of little-known facts about bird migrations. I had no idea then that birding would become important in something eventually entitled "eco-tourism."

Life was not totally idyllic. Rob's former wife sued Winnie for alienation of affections. No one could remember when such a suit had last been filed. Spectators arrived early to get seats in the courtroom. The classic beauty of the woman and the prankish wit of the jovial defendant made it the best show in town.

I covered the story. Rob, who never wanted publicity, didn't crave it now, but he knew that this was something I had to do and felt no personal resentment. I quoted Rob's one-liners and described the innocent smile on Winnie's face as she looked affectionately at her husband on the witness stand.

It so happened that another trial, a child-custody case involving a prominent family of the area, was being held in the Nueces County courthouse at the same time. This case had such newsworthy elements as the seducer climbing up onto a balcony for clandestine meetings.

Also, national news services were carrying stories of the deliciously wicked movie star Errol Flynn, caught making love with nothing on but his shoes. Sex was being headlined day after day. At that time, sex was something newspapers usually ignored.

Bob Jackson, a circumspect editor on the *Caller-Times*, had finally had enough. He thumbtacked a notice on the newspaper bulletin board: "There will be no more bedroom scenes on the front page unless they involve either the Pope or Eleanor Roosevelt."

It was all over, anyhow, where Rob and Winnie were concerned. Jurors in the alienation of affections case, drawn into the magnetic field of the femininity of the woman and the machismo of the man, took hardly any time to deliberate and found the defendants innocent.

A few years later, Rob died. He stipulated before his death that he wanted to be cremated and have his ashes scattered on the waters of Apalachicola Bay, where he first went to sea. One of his sons arrived soon after Rob's death and said he'd take the ashes. He was scheduled to make a business trip to New Orleans, and he said he would go on from there to Apalachicola.

Winnie was a wise woman. She made no protest. She went to the funeral home and stood guard, waiting until the ashes were put into an urn. Taking the urn in her arms, she caught the first plane for Florida. Standing alone on a bridge she and Rob had sailed under on *Rusty* many times, Winnie quietly committed Rob's ashes to the sea.

14
Progress Be Damned

It is possible that I was one of the early writers in the environmental movement and didn't even know it. I had never heard the word *ecology* until I met Joel Hedgpeth, a marine biologist who was in Rockport working on his doctorate while I was working on the *Rockport Pilot* newspaper. With Joel, I had a whole new environment to learn and write about: science and what it was teaching us about the survival of the planet.

Joel had grown up in Walnut Creek, California and his intellect was such that he didn't fit in easily with everyday Texans. Later, he would speak of the time he spent in Rockport as his "years of exile." He found this coast to be "unlettered and a boorish cultural void."

His attitudes probably resulted from a childhood that isolated him. He had picked up a dynamite cap in the California hills. It exploded, injuring him severely. When I knew him, a goatee partially covered scars on his face, and I could only guess at the scars left on his heart by other children who must have mocked him while his face was being reshaped with plastic surgery.

Joel spoke in sardonic tones, much as a villain would say his lines in a melodrama. He used words that I often had to look up in the dictionary, but those words flowed out of him as artlessly as

Joel Hedgpeth.

Progress Be Damned 61

those from a child's mouth. His candid comments could and did cut deeply, but they were totally honest. He was, although he didn't want anyone to know it, really kind and loving. Something inside each of us reached out to the other, and we were friends, despite barriers he put up to prevent me or anybody else from getting close to him.

As a reporter, I recognized that here was a man who could open up to me a new understanding of our bays and shores. He had a quirky sense of humor, and I thought it was a joke when he told me he was president of the International Society for the Prevention of Progress. With me, he was patient, giving me a basic course in environmental science.

Progress to me had always been a good thing, what you strove to promote in news documentaries. The building of dams in South Texas was considered a huge injection of life-giving water for economic development. Joel taught me that there was an entirely different way of looking at things. I learned what damage is done to life that depended upon the watershed when a dam is built. I was cognizant for the first time of how industrial and agricultural discharges pollute water and air.

Joel and Dr. Gordon Gunter were working in Rockport for Texas Parks and Wildlife, studying plankton and microscopic sea life. They would go from Rockport to Mustang Island to establish the University of Texas Marine Science Center. From there, Joel would return to the West Coast, working first at Scripps Institute, and later heading up the marine science department of the University of Oregon in Newport.

He left me with a frame of mind that would enable me to write extensively about our coastal resources and to work with the Council of Governments' Environmental Quality Committee. That committee, made up of environmentalists and industrialists, searched for balance that would avoid long-term damage to the environment yet interfere as little as possible with the economy that provides a living for human beings.

Friends in the news business liked to come from Corpus Christi to Rockport for weekends. We'd cross the causeway to Goose Island and sit below Big Tree, a thousand-year-old treasure of a live oak. Joel played an Irish harp and would sing to us Welsh ballads from his own heritage, romantic songs from Broadway shows, and light opera or dirty ditties.

I had no idea how universal Joel's ideas on the environment that I wrote about then would become in this country.

In California, Joel has became one of the most highly respected marine biologists of the nation. I read from time to time of papers he is giving at an international meeting. I see him now and then on public television, talking about preventing damage to San Francisco Bay or to the Galapagos Islands.

I'm sure I was not the only writer he reached to help raise awareness of environmental sciences. His ideas are now mainstream. I believe he had an important part in making them that way in the nation.

15
Downriver

Inevitably, people gain a different understanding of the world to which they are accustomed if they live a few years in another culture. This is especially crucial for a reporter.

One of the men I had dated in Angleton was Buckley Wright. He went overseas, fought on the European front, and was among the troops who went into Paris when it was liberated. In France, he began drinking heavily and would later become an alcoholic. I thought nothing about his drinking at the time, as nearly everyone I knew drank too much. Buckley and I wrote regularly and agreed to marry. I met him in San Antonio when he was released from service. We married and took part in that joyous frenzy of flagwaving and welcoming the troops when they came marching home. Buckley signed a contract with an oil company to go to Colombia for two years.

I couldn't wait for the chance to experience life in another country. I made contact with various publications for whom I would be a news stringer. A British aviation writer I had met at a navy party, Keith Ayling, arranged for his agent, Nancy Parker, to represent me as a freelance writer.

The first months in Colombia, I lived behind a high fence in a cluster of company houses in Barrancabermeja. Almost everyone living in the encampment was from Sonya, Ontario. The Canadians were congenial, and our lives pleasant, with live-in servants and morning, luncheon, afternoon, and evening bridge games.

I had little to do with the running of our house except to write in the commissary book what food we needed to have delivered. The one thing my competent maid, Maria, could not do was read and write. She planned, cooked, and served our meals, and scrubbed down the tile floors and stucco walls every day as though they were infected with the plague.

All company cars were Model B Fords, but she could recognize the driver of any car approaching. If a guest arrived who was the wife of one of the top company executives, she served delicacies on our best china. If the family was of no importance in Maria's eyes, the guest might be served a stale muffin on a cracked plate. Nothing I could do about it.

Almost the only local culture I encountered inside the complex was the iguana. The big lizards were as reluctant as I to dispute right-of-way. When we met in a path, we stopped, looked each other over, then politely detoured, each leaving the other ample room.

Buckley was transferred downriver in 1946. This meant we would live in small company stations where we would be the only North Americans. There was a definite difference in company treatment of United States citizens and those of Colombia. One of the most obvious differences was that we lived in "first-class houses." Three Colombian employees and their families lived in houses designated as "second class." Our compound was near a small village.

Buckley was away on business most of the time. I was free to explore and write. There were no roads as such. Travel through the jungle was possible only in a jeep with men walking ahead of the jeep cutting a path with machetes. A net enveloped us if we drove into nearby mountains. Indians there lived as though this were the Stone Age and shot poison arrows at intruders.

Travel on the river was by paddle-wheel boat, dugout canoe, or commercial power launches.

Paddle-wheel boats pulled a barge behind them, on which were cows, lambs, and chickens. By looking to see what had disappeared from the barge each day, you knew what to expect for dinner.

I traveled with the Colombians whenever possible. On one

trip, some of my neighbors and I made our way to a road up a high mountain to Ocaña. We booked passage and rode up in the back of a pickup truck. This mountain town was known for the volatility of its people. A sign in a restaurant said, "Religion and politics may not be discussed here." Such conversations ended in fights that left broken chairs and tables.

Two young boys guided me on a tour of the city. I covered my head respectfully when we went into the cathedral, as we all did at that time upon entering an Episcopal church. Episcopalians in the United States are considered Protestant, but elsewhere in the world they are considered Anglican Catholic. The boys, having established that I was an Episcopalian, said, "There are two of your countrymen living in this city. We are sure you would not want to know them because they are Protestants." I assumed a proper expression of horror and forewent that opportunity.

Later, back on the riverbank, a dugout canoe provided transportation to the scene when the mysterious jungle wireless spread the word that a plane had crashed not too far away, causing multiple deaths. I was asked to cover the crash story for *Time* magazine. Accurate information was, as always, difficult to learn here. These were not people who compiled data or accurate statistics. There were no official sources. I questioned whomever I could.

"How many people were killed?"

"Oh, maybe twenty, or thirty; maybe forty, or maybe fifty."

Frustrated, I tried to rely on those closest to the scene. A telegraph operator in a tent nearby sent my final story out of the jungle to *Time*.

On the same day that I expected the South American edition of the magazine to arrive with my story in it, I learned that one of my informants had been wrong. The plane I wrote about did not belong to the company to which I had attributed ownership.

The next day, a company plane brought our mail, including a letter from *Time*. It contained an apology, saying that my story was pushed out at the last minute to make room for a story on a major revolution that broke out in another South American country. The letter contained a check for my story that did not run. I felt guilty cashing it. More than that, I felt thankful for an undeserved break; my mistake never saw print.

Remarkably, these men and women had almost no awareness of

the world outside their immediate environs. They were incredulous when I told them there were bodies of water in the world other than the Magdelena River. No sound of the bombing and blasting of World War II had been heard here. None of the communist influence evident in urban areas of Colombia had reached the jungle stations.

Wild orchids and multicolored flowers hung from shrubs and branches of trees. Eyes of brightly painted parrots tracked me as I walked paths where underbrush had been cut away. At a junction of two paths, I saw the track of a large animal's paw. My camera was hanging over my shoulder, and I shot a picture. An elderly man coming along the path stopped to watch me.

"*Tigre*," he said, and I agreed. He had never seen a camera before. I explained, as best I could, the basics of photography to him.

He held out his hand and asked to see the picture I had taken. I told him condescendingly that film had to be processed in a laboratory before pictures could be developed. With no preconceived ideas, his mind was open to a possibility that did not occur to me. A few years later, when a camera was introduced that had its own processing system built in, I remembered the old man whom I had considered to be ignorant, and my own unimaginative response to his concept. This reporter was learning.

Each week, a company seaplane landed on the river, dodging women washing their clothes on rocks, and brought mail and whatever supplies we had ordered the previous week, canned goods, staples, and dried milk. The company plane carried back to Cartagena whatever I had written to mail to Nancy Parker or to newspapers.

Much of our food was made up of imported and expensive canned goods flown from the commissary. Colombian residents could not afford that luxury but could live off the fruit of the land, including platanos and coconuts. When I wanted a coconut, I called the security guard, who walked around the houses with a machete in his hand twenty-four hours a day.

Christmas came. Nothing in the jungle looked like a Christmas tree, but I had a machete-wielder cut down a fairly well-shaped tree of unidentified species. By the time I made paper ornaments and trimmed the tree, it had died and drooped exhaustedly. It was not what you would call a traditional *Natividad*, but it served as the subject of a humor article that Nancy Parker sold to *Holiday* magazine, so there was something to celebrate.

Shortly before I left South America, my mother came to visit me. A woman with Victorian manners, she found there a society she had not known existed. She was shocked to find out that the only wedding dresses sold in the village were maternity dresses. The church charged so much to perform a wedding ceremony that no one could afford it. However, the wedding was free if the woman was pregnant. The priest in the village wandered down paths in his flowing robes with his woman and children parading behind him.

Native women would come up and touch my mother, saying in amazement, "*Que entero*," which means "how entire." She had her own teeth and a youthful vigor. There, women were old by the age of forty.

While Buckley was away traveling, Mother helped me realize that his drinking problem was too serious for me to ingnore and convinced me to return home with her.

On the way back home, Mother and I flew to Bogotá, then Medellín. We were enraptured by this then-beautiful city, which would later become the country's drug capital. Flying on to Aruba, we boarded a Standard Oil tanker. The son of one of Mother's friends had arranged for us to return to the United States as passengers.

Although I was to spend time with Buckley later in Venezuela, there proved to be nothing that I could do about his drinking, and by the end of 1949, Buckley and I were divorced. I returned to Corpus Christi hoping to reestablish old contacts.

My experiences in South America made me question whether people living a primitive life are happier than those in the world of technology, consumption, and stress. Whatever I wrote in the future would be with a broader vision, with new definitions of the words "normal" and "newsworthy" and "happiness."

16
Wavelengths

Back in Corpus Christi, there was an important development in my life. Medical science was advancing rapidly. Dr. Robert Thomason was able to diagnose the illness with which I had lived since I was five years old as undulant fever. Injections for the next year brought it under control. I no longer lost consciousness and suddenly dropped to the ground to the trepidation of whoever was nearby.

Having lived in South America for the last few years, I had only a strange assortment of tropical clothes. Before I even had time to buy a new suit and begin job interviews, I ran into former police chief Earl Dunn, who offered to create a position for me as news director of a new commercial radio station that he had recently established with three partners. Radio was about to come into its own.

When I reported to work, Earl told me that he needed a little time to bring the partners into agreement about the importance of shaping this form of communication with news content. I agreed to work in other capacities while this was accomplished. I read wire news on the air and did a spontaneous, humorous talk program with one of the announcers.

Shortly after Christmas, Ben, the program director, brought me some advertising material and asked me to write commercials selling Christmas gifts. He told me I should certify the times and dates that the commercials had run on the station early in December.

Puzzled, I asked him, "What gives?"

"This is co-op advertising," he explained. "A national or regional wholesaler and a local retailer each agree to pay half the cost of the time. The commercials never run, but the wholesaler doesn't know that. We bill him for his half, and the radio station splits that money with the retailer."

"That's fraud," I said incredulously.

"Where you been, gal? Everybody does it. No big deal. Things aren't that unequivocal."

I had learned in Angleton that business was not always conducted in the way that I had been brought up to believe it was. This was still hard for me to accept.

Clyde, one of the announcers, was experimenting with something else new, audiotapes. The station had bought a tape recorder, about the size of a footlocker, much too heavy for me to carry. One day, we heard that a boat had sunk, and people were drowning off Indian Point at Portland.

Clyde said, "Come on. We'll go tape a description of the rescue." We rushed over there. It was too late. Whatever had happened, there was no one there and nothing going on. With no hesitation, Clyde set up the equipment and began speaking into a mike, describing all the drama of a tragedy at sea. I already knew I wanted no more involvement with any of this.

Earl came to me about that time and told me that he was unable to persuade his partners to assume the expense of a local news operation. They wanted me to stay on in the program department, which I declined. I knew that Earl himself was honest. He was in charge of engineering at the station and was totally unaware of the way programming and advertising were being handled.

Buddy, an announcer at another radio station, KSIX, suggested I apply for work there. I quizzed him, and he assured me that Vann M. Kennedy, who owned controlling stock in and was manager of KSIX, was a highly principled person.

I applied and was invited to an interview. Mr. Kennedy and I had an animated conversation of several hours. I expected him to make me an offer. Weeks passed, and he didn't.

Buddy and I went to the Padre Island beach on an outing one

weekend. Returning to Corpus Christi, he stopped the car in a service station. While we were getting gasoline, he noticed that Mr. Kennedy—"the Colonel," as Buddy called him—was in another part of the station.

I was wearing shorts and a halter and was barefoot, but I didn't have anything to lose. I got out of the car, walked over, and greeted Mr. Kennedy. He responded as formally as though we were meeting for high tea. We exchanged pleasantries, and I started to walk off. Stopping me, he asked, "Would you still like to go to work for me?" I said yes, and he instructed, "Come to work Monday morning."

I later learned that he had not hired me when I applied because his strict standards did not allow him to pirate personnel from a competing station. I had resigned and was unemployed when I approached him in the service station, so he felt free to hire me. After I knew that, I was sure that I was where I belonged, working for a man doing business conscientiously.

In these last years of the twentieth century, much of the public has lost faith in the integrity of not only government but also of business. What we once took for granted, that affairs of state and commerce are conducted honorably, is now celebrated as exceptional when it is recognized.

17
Sky High

At times in my life, everything was going so well for me that I felt I was truly riding "sky high." This was especially true when radio was the town crier, the communicator that reached everyone, before television barged its way in. My exhilaration was topped off when I flew with the Blue Angels, the navy aerobatics team that performs for air shows across the nation.

Lieutenant Commander Dick Newhafer obtained permission for me to fly with him when the team was rehearsing aerobatics for a show in Corpus Christi—never to be called stunts.

Arriving at the appointed hour, I saw that Dick was taking oxygen. He grinned at me, because everybody knew oxygen was great for a hangover.

All the jets in the formation on the ground were single-seaters except for his, a TV-2 that carried a passenger behind the pilot. Dick helped me into the rear seat and gave me a helmet with a built-in microphone. We talked on an intercom, our conversation live and taped.

This was what I loved about radio: It was so simple, and you took your listeners with you as you went. No waiting for newspaper presses to roll or styling my hair for appearance before the cameras. This was instantaneous and intimate.

Dick Newhafer and Juliet.

    We took off in a formation of planes flown by some of the most skilled pilots in the navy. Dick explained every maneuver as we flew low and high, banking steeply, looping, stalling. Wings almost kissed as jets crisscrossed, passed one another, and doubled back over the mainland, the barrier islands, then the sea.
    We were so high that the surface of the earth appeared much as it would years later in pictures shot from satellites. Each plane went into a spin, faster and faster. Dick pulled us out when it seemed to me we were only feet off the ground. I couldn't see what was happening to the other planes in the formation because I could not raise my head. With my chin on my chest, I was unable to talk into the mike.

Dick, comfortable in his pressure suit, chatted right along as though he intended this to be a monologue. When I recovered sufficiently to raise my head and adjust the mike, my first words were in a high and squeaky voice. I giggled. Atmospheric intoxication.

As exciting as this flight was, I was even more excited in my new job. Vann M. Kennedy named me news director of KSIX, opening up limitless opportunities.

Corpus Christi was growing. Heavy industry lined the ship channel for miles. Yet this remained a uniquely clean port town, with a sparkling bayfront. That buzz word tourism was flying around in the heads of local government officials and business leaders. Later, Corpus Christi would lose momentum, but at that point in time, nothing could stop it.

I became a one-woman news bureau in a city with a population of 130,000. Every day I made trips to the police station, city hall, and the courthouse. A police radio scanner behind my desk sent out constant signals that I tuned my ear to only if I heard the code for something major. By telephone, I contacted emergency service providers, spokesmen for organizations active in the city, and an ever-growing list of news sources.

Trying not to let any stories fall through the cracks, I covered important events at the scene whenever they happened. By every noontime, I had as many as thirty stories written, each thirty to ninety seconds long. By six o'clock, noon stories had been updated and new stories written. A summary of the local news of the day was compiled for ten o'clock. In my free time, I made documentaries and wrote in-depth stories to run as news specials.

It would not have been possible without a network of news sources who called me with information or tips. Included were friends of my parents, friends of mine from while I was in school in Corpus Christi, and other contacts that I worked to develop each day.

Newspapers, thank goodness, still carry a variety of stories at some length. Some do a better job than others of making sure that what could be called "quiet news of importance" has an audience. Radio, which I felt really gave the reporter the freedom to go into depth, now offers little more than a list of headlines.

As news director at the station, I felt that it was demanded of me to put a story into context so that the listener could discover why it had happened and what significance it had. At that time, before television took over and radio was pushed into the background, I was still convinced it was possible to give listeners a good enough understanding of the news so that they could apply it to their own lives and communities.

Distinctions were still made between reporting facts and offering commentary or expressing opinions. Reporters, like anyone else, had strong opinions. Among those I knew, most were able to give a fair account. We also kept in mind that we could be wrong in what we had concluded and might have to rethink a situation when there was new information.

Reporters were alert to any dubious conduct on the part of public officials and did not hesitate to probe, but we were not adversarial. We were polite and accepted as a part of the system. Reporters and news sources shared an interest in making government work and in informing the public accurately, not sensationally.

18
Sound of the Siren

Many reporters are intoxicated by the crime beat in their first years on the street. The addiction usually moderates with time; however, I doubt that there are many crime reporters who ever hear the sound of the siren without a vestigial urge, however gentle, to go to the scene.

When I hear the sound most clearly, I think of two retired navy men, one a noncommissioned officer, a chief, and the other an admiral, who retired as commanding officer of the naval base in Corpus Christi.

Admiral Joe Dunn and John Carlisle had much in common. They treated all comers in exactly the same way, fairly and according to law, with no privilege for wealth or political clout.

Reporters had never, in their most fanciful moments, conceived of having such cooperative public officials as news sources. Neither man hesitated to answer questions truthfully, feared losing his job, or worried about his popularity.

Both stood up for their men, at least in public. They might have been quite punitive in calling the men to task later in the privacy of an office.

Admiral Joe Dunn was director of the city's Department of

Public Safety for a memorable period in the fifties. He was accustomed to unquestioned respect.

The *Caller-Times* frequently expressed the opinion editorially that the position of Director of Public Safety should be abolished as an unnecessary expense. On news pages, every time Admiral Dunn's name was mentioned, the amount of his salary was written after his name, in the way that newspapers frequently write a person's age, set off in commas.

Admiral Dunn had no intention of ordering or allowing offenses of prominent citizens to be covered up. He saw to it that services in an elite part of the city were on no different level from those in middle- or low-income neighborhoods.

Fire Chief John Carlisle had been a navy firefighter and had joined the Corpus Christi force immediately after World War II. He did not have the social position or graces of Admiral Dunn, but he knew himself and his job and looked neither up to nor down on any man. John was chief of the Corpus Christi firefighting force for over thirty years, from 1946 until 1979.

John pursued arson no matter whose brother-in-law was looking for a way to get out of an unsuccessful business and collect insurance. Developers and builders were horrified to find that they couldn't skimp on electrical systems or hurricane-wind-resistant construction. They were required to get in line with codes and standards.

John stayed as far away from city hall as possible. His wife wanted to build a new home. He made a good salary, but he told her, in his own ingratiating way, "Hell, no! I don't want house payments. Then I got to worry about keeping my job, and to do that, I got to kiss ass at city hall."

John was the kind of man who always went into a dangerous situation first and led his men. His right-hand man, Andrew Ordner, loved the chief dearly but was quite fearful of him and was forever under stress.

Ordner had ulcers. His doctor told him that he would never be well unless he learned to stand up to the chief. The mild-mannered fireman went to the door of John's office, stood there getting up courage, then, in a loud, shaking voice, declaimed, "Go to Hell!"

John looked up from his paperwork in amazement, figured out that Ordner was asserting himself, and burst out laughing.

Ordner gave a loud sigh of relief. He never had another ulcer, and John enjoyed telling the story until the day he died.

The admiral called John "the Blaster," because his voice was so loud, and he called me "the Leaping Gazelle," because I was so adept at jumping fire hoses when flames were about to trap me in a confined area.

The admiral's office was in city hall, and he attended council meetings regularly. His mere presence made the staff and elected officials nervous, because what he said was never politically correct. When someone came to a council meeting complaining about the actions of police officers, the admiral listened with attention. If he recognized half-truths and misrepresentations, he would draw himself up to military stance and, in a voice often used to address the troops, demand, "What do you want, sir, baked pig with apple in mouth?"

If complaints were about the admiral himself, he could handle that with a pleasant smile on the side of his face turned to the audience. From the other side of his mouth, he would say to me, "I feel like a bastard at the family reunion."

One morning, the admiral and I were drinking coffee in his office looking out over the luminous waters of the bay. We were talking about the future of government if elected officials continually backed off from what needed to be done to placate those whose favor they feared losing.

"It requires a certain amount of fortitude," the admiral said, "to repel the pressure of the powerful and listen to all the naysayers drone on, yet stick with your own wisdom."

"What gives a person strength?" I asked him.

"You have to believe in yourself, then know that you are an integral part of the universe. You have to believe good things can happen in the entirety of it, even if you are damn disgusted because you can't control the world and make it do what you want it to do."

"Are we losing that strength because people don't have the kind of faith they once had?"

"Everybody has faith. If we didn't, we wouldn't dare go to sea in a ship. You have to realize, most people have good intentions. Most of us don't intend to lie, steal, or murder."

I nodded. "I believe that. For instance, the murder last night — "

"What murder?" The admiral's big, muscular figure came out of his leather chair. "I checked with the police chief earlier, and he told me nothing happened last night."

He picked up the phone and called Chief Dick Runyon. With a voice full of controlled venom, he asserted, "Juliet says there was a murder last night."

Runyon replied, "It was just a routine murder. One Mexican stabbed another in a bar."

His control slipping, the admiral roared into the telephone in a voice that could have been heard over the din of jets taking off from the flight deck of a carrier, "There will be no routine murders in Corpus Christi!"

There were, of course; much as there were many fires, no matter how hard John worked to prevent them, preaching his constant theme: "Nothing is fireproof, only fire-resistant."

Disasters seldom happen at a convenient time. One afternoon, I was attending a cocktail party for some visiting travel writers on the top floor of the Plaza Hotel. Looking out a window, I saw a huge expanse of black smoke with treacherous entrails of flames. A wildfire was spreading through the Southwestern Oil and Refining Company tank farm.

I drove as close as I could get to the fire, ditched my car, then ran across the farm on high heels, wearing my party dress with an ankle-length skirt. One of the firemen was running near me. A tall wire fence got in our way. He threw me over the fence, then hurdled it himself.

All available fire companies in the area had been called in. The fire had started with the explosion of a tank containing nearly sixty thousand barrels of kerosene. The effort was to try to prevent the spread of the flames.

I found a telephone in a small office building near a large tank. This was immediately before the days of television. My calls from the tank farm went on the air, patched through the control board at the KSIX radio studio by the announcer on duty. The radio station stayed on all night because the fire threatened the city.

In the early-morning hours, the firefighters ran out of foam. John had foreseen this and had called Houston. A truckload of foam was on the way. Until it arrived, there wasn't much anybody could do. I went home long enough to change clothes, then rejoined fire chiefs from all around South Texas, who sat in a circle on empty foam cans while their men patrolled the tank farm and reported to them.

Then it happened. A tremendous blast shook the ground for miles around. Only a few yards from where we sat, a mushroom cloud arose that looked much like pictures I had seen of atom bombs. The tank closest to us had boiled over, launching a gaseous fireball into the air, hot as the core of the earth.

These things we learned later. At the moment of the boil-over, everybody ran mindlessly from the unbearable sound and heat. We ran as though aimed through the barrel of a cannon, not by our own volition. I have no memory of running, only of the eruption. When awareness returned to me, I was lying on the ground under a house, as was a marine I had never seen before. Each of us sized up the other, our eyes asking, "Are we alive or dead?"

John was on the fire-system radio, checking with stations he had posted for many blocks in the radius of the tank farm. He accounted for all the firefighters who had been sitting in that circle. Then he asked whether anyone knew where I was. An officer stationed four blocks from the blast responded, "I don't know where she is now, Chief, but she looked fine when she ran by here."

When we were reunited at the tank farm, I found that the office in which I had been using the telephone was blown away. It was first daylight when the truckload of foam arrived from Houston. The truck stopped, and one tire burst into flames. The vehicle had been traveling so fast and had come to such a sudden halt that the rubber ignited. Our tension broke when this silly little fire licked out at us from the wheel. With the foam and renewed energy, firemen rushed back into action in the tank farm.

Seventeen hours had passed before the blaze was controlled and I limped away. We had not lost a man. All that was lost were many millions of dollars in petroleum products, expensive foam, and John's voice, which had been used up screaming through his bullhorn.

At fires, John bellowed at all of us, but he did so because fast action was necessary for our protection. It didn't matter who was on the scene, the mayor, the county judge, or a newspaper publisher, when John gave an order sandwiched in between some of his choice cuss words, everybody said snappily, "Yes, sir."

Years after the tank-farm fire, the admiral was dead and John was in the hospital, where he learned that he was dying. He called Bill Walraven, columnist, Texas historian, and humorist. In Bill's reporting days, John had saved his life as often as he did mine by blasting us away from danger with his bullhorn.

In what was left of that legendary voice, John said, "Bill, I want you to write my obituary." Walraven did so, took it to the hospital, and let John read it; he laughed all the way through. He made a few corrections, then said, "That's great." A few days later, he died.

His funeral was in First Baptist Church on Ocean Drive. The huge nave of the church was completely filled with people accustomed to looking solemn and suffering through funerals. Walraven read the obituary, page after page, with all the stories of the chief tottering on a roof collapsing as flames rose through it. Every hilarious tale had a happy ending.

The eulogy itself had a moral. "With good lungs and enough guts, you *can* beat city hall." I never have laughed so hard at a funeral. I cried a lot, too.

There are few department heads like the admiral and John around city halls today. Their kind of guy has been replaced by the adroit who know how to smooth the way for special interests and make government comfortable for both elected officials and bureaucrats. City hall is much less fun to cover now.

19
The Oil Editor

I can think of nothing more satisfying than hearing someone who has shared similar experiences, who is knowledgeable and analytical, express the same conclusions at which I have arrived. Nancy Heard was a woman who validated ideas for me, giving me incentives to proceed in ways that I found right for me.

Some women were coming into news with strong demands for equality. Others were flirtatious, taking advantage of their femininity. Nancy and I reserved our identities as women for our private lives; at work we were unmodified reporters. A world of women do that today, but in 1954, when Nancy and I met, it was not commonplace.

In those years, few women in the news business received the same recognition and respect given men. Nancy Heard was one of those few. She was oil editor of the *Caller-Times*.

The adolescent oil industry was one of the last places a woman could expect to find equality. Yet oilmen from all over the state put their trust in Nancy as they did in no other writer. Her intelligence was a balance of information and knowledge with rational thought and unusual compassion. She was a tough professional, but as a private citizen, she took great responsibility for helping her fellow human beings whenever she could.

It didn't detract from the oilmen's interest in her that she was one of the best-looking women around. Her facial features were delicate but strong, and brown hair with gold streaks curled randomly around her head. She didn't deliberately use her looks, but they couldn't be denied.

Executive secretaries in oil company offices would tell her, "Go out with so-and-so. He always leaves a hundred-dollar bill on the bureau." Nancy left the secretaries guessing, but the oilmen knew exactly where she drew the line.

When I bought a house for the first time, she and I lived together there. She was as good a housekeeper as a reporter, cooking wholesome meals for us and cleaning where it had not occurred to me dirt would exist. She even washed the leaves of houseplants with soap and water.

Nancy celebrated life. She loved holidays. At Christmas she strung cranberries and popcorn for the tree. Sometimes the needle pricked and the popcorn was as red as the cranberries, if we had drunk a bit too much holiday cheer. We painted "Merry Christmas and Happy New Year" in big letters across the front of the house. Never mind that that we'd have to sand and repaint the house when the New Year arrived.

With her, I would learn the inside story of the oil industry and of the lives of the free-spending oilmen. Money came easily out of the ground and slid away as effortlessly into dry holes. This fueled a religion of "spend it before you lose it." Nancy was writing technical articles that were important to everyone in the industry across the state. I was finding stories of general interest to television viewers eager to follow the drama of this boom-time chase of the oil dollar. After the work was done, we dined, danced, and enjoyed the playtime that was as much a part of the oil patch tradition as the big discovery wells.

She told me about John Toudouze, with whom she had fallen in love when she was working on a newspaper in Carlsbad, New Mexico, before she came to Corpus Christi. He was from an old San Antonio family and was selling oil-field supplies. Their engagement had broken off when Nancy put her work first.

She rarely took a day to play but had finally agreed to go on a picnic in the mountains with John so they would have time for one another. A plane crashed nearby, and she spent the day on the tele-

Juliet with Nancy Heard.

phone providing news to various sources. Every newswoman can relate to that. News never breaks at a convenient time or on a predetermined schedule. John and Nancy argued and split.

One night months later, while Nancy and I were living together, a tall, slender man with a big smile and a slow drawl walked into our house. Immediately, the atmosphere in the room was so rare that it was like breathing pure oxygen. This was John Toudouze. It was inevitable. She married him. The *San Antonio Express* grabbed her as oil editor.

She and John raised two adopted children, Melissa and Paul. A child of their own, Sara, was born on the day that the United States Marines landed in Lebanon. Nancy didn't know about the landing for three days, because she was in a coma near death. That was the only time I ever knew her to be unaware of a big breaking news story.

She survived, but her health had deteriorated after years of sleeping too little, smoking and drinking too much, and working and playing with a body-blasting dynamism.

While Sara was still a baby, one of Nancy's lungs collapsed. The doctor said Nancy could live no more than five years. She said, "I'll live until Sara is grown." She did, making an eventful life for Sara and the two older children while working at the oil desk as long as she was able.

She told me, "When I'm dead, put me in a plastic bag out on the curb for the garbage man to pick up. Who cares. While I'm alive, we'll make the most of it."

We did. We put her in a wheelchair and took in the Texas Hemisfair. We listened to Sara play the piano as her talent became more and more evident. We all talked, usually at the kitchen table, hour after hour, even when Nancy had to gasp for breath to speak. She was a person with solutions rather than complaints, seeing novel ways to make substantive and farsighted changes in our society.

When she could no longer get out of bed, she stayed on the telephone, soliciting support for the political organization Common Cause, determined to leave behind a government better than the one she had known.

Whenever I wonder whether hard work on a news story or time spent trying to improve government is worth it, I think of

Nancy. Nobody could convince her that she was the only one who cared or that she couldn't make a difference.

Nancy had fidelity to news coverage and honest government. So did Sara, who developed into a brilliant and mature young woman. Nancy had said she would live until her youngest daughter was grown. A few weeks after Sara graduated from college, Nancy died. She seldom reneged on a commitment.

20

The FCC Hearing

In the summer of 1956, my colleague Walter Furley and I got on a plane for Washington, D.C., to meet Vann Kennedy and reporter Gene Looper to testify in a hearing before a Federal Communications Commission examiner. We were among three applicants for a television license in Corpus Christi.

On the plane, we were still working on exhibits that would be put into evidence. Much of our case was based on promise and performance under our radio license, so we searched radio logs to verify every news special and public service program for which we could take credit. We honestly believed that we could serve the community to a greater degree with this new miracle of communication. We had no idea how different from radio the demands, constraints, and costs of television would be.

By the time Walter and I reached Washington, we had slept little and eaten erratically for many hours. I took the stand with my eyes watering, my ear canals blocked so that it was hard for me to hear, and with no voice, only a croak.

I had been a witness before, in change-of-venue hearings and before federal and state grand juries, to testify about what I had learned in crime reporting and what I had broadcast. In those set-

The FCC Hearing 87

tings, the atmosphere was relaxed. I was answering impersonally questions put to me by judges and attorneys who were friends.

The FCC hearing, conducted by an examiner, was held in a room with spokesmen for the two applicants competing with us for the license. Their attorneys, seven of them, were taking deadly aim at every word I said, trying to confuse or discredit me, and often succeeding. Fortunately, our attorneys were as good as theirs, and they pulled me out of every hole into which I dug myself.

Actually, all the attorneys had a hard time concentrating on what I was saying. Sitting in the courtroom was the lead witness for the competing Tulsa station. She was a scintillating brunette whose necklines plunged a little lower each day. I resembled a schoolgirl fresh from the convent, wearing a navy blue suit with a white Peter Pan collar.

The first part of my testimony was positive, telling of our past accomplishments on radio and what we proposed for television. Our programming, I declared, would give South Texas, with its high illiteracy rate and low income level, exposure to the finest entertainment and educational programs. Such an uninformed view! Nothing forewarned me of sitcoms and tabloid news.

The next part of my testimony was offensive to me. I had to testify to the malfeasance of two of the men involved in the applications of our competitors. Both were my friends, and we were eye-to-eye there in the room.

One of them was Edgar Linkenhoger, always helpful to me as a reporter. He was a good friend of Lyndon Johnson and had been awarded profitable contracts through that connection. He had a number of businesses, including construction companies and a truck line.

This is where knowledge I had acquired as a ten-year-old observing my father's trucking business paid off. Having witnessed the collusion of truck lines and railroad commissioners as a child, it was easy for me to find public records that would expose Linkenhoger's small-time dealings in Texas. Court records showed his company had been found guilty of and fined for overloading trucks about nine hundred times.

I also went to the records of the city building official. There I found numerous small fines for convictions on violations of building codes. Such fines cost much less than meeting building standards. No attempt was made to refute the information, as I had copies of the records.

When court recessed, Linkenhoger came over and hugged me. Laughing, he said, "You did a damn good job." He was that kind of a fellow. He did what he thought he had to do to succeed in business, and he did not resent the fact that I did what I thought I had to do as a part of my job. He was one of many people I knew and liked who were not hypocritical and made no attempt to be something they weren't, those I distinguished from other, less forthcoming, friends as "honest crooks."

The other person I reluctantly shredded in testimony was Allan Dale. He had worked at various times on radio in the Rio Grande Valley and as an announcer at KSIX, where we got to know one another.

In an exhibit entered into the hearing record, Allan described at length a call-in program that he created and conducted on the air when he was in the Valley. This program, as it was detailed, was much like the vitriolic talk shows made popular years later by Rush Limbaugh, which incite listeners to vent their rage against life's inequities, particularly those that can be blamed on the government.

Following the trail that a radio personality leaves on program logs and in newspaper radio guides, I made a discovery. No such program ever appeared in a log or guide where Allan had worked. I interviewed station personnel who had been his colleagues in the Valley. They told me that Allan had envisioned such a program, was always talking about it, but had never been able to persuade a station to put it on the air. It was his dream.

Allan's only crime was a slight problem of perjury in the hearing exhibit, claiming community benefits and results from a program that had never aired. In later years, he did go on the air with such a call-in program, which received good ratings at a San Antonio radio station.

Gene Looper followed me to the stand. One of the questions he was asked by an opposing attorney was, "How much classical music does KSIX radio carry?"

Looper gave figures showing that the amount of classical music was substantial.

The lawyer then asked, "How many people in the Corpus Christi area are devotees of classical music?"

The FCC Hearing 89

"Very few," Looper replied frankly.

The adversary had hoped to show that KSIX did not respond to the interests of listeners. This backfired. The hearing examiner spoke into the record, "It is good to know that a station has the fortitude to consider something other than ratings and schedule programs elevating to the community."

Mr. Kennedy spent seven days on the stand and needed neither our attorneys nor the examiner to help him out. His answers to every question were so thorough and well-documented that no one could find any way to trip him up.

The charming brunette, testifying for her applicant, had a problem that fell into the same category as the one Allan had. She had testified that she herself wrote the code of ethics set out in the application for the station license. Mary Kennedy thought the words in the code sounded familiar. She did some quick research and found that the code in the competing station's application was word for word like the NBC code. Walter Furley stayed up all night writing an entirely new exhibit to give the full implication of this discovery.

It was the last exhibit that our attorneys presented. They then recalled the woman with the winning ways to the stand and again asked her, "Did you yourself write this code of ethics?"

She replied, "Every word of it."

The new exhibit was then presented to the examiner. His gavel came down, and the hearing was over.

Finally, we were awarded a license for what was then KSIX-TV, later changed to KZTV. Furthermore, the exhibits that Mr. Kennedy had masterminded are considered so superior that those seeking licenses from any part of the nation study them as a model to this day.

We weren't home free. One competitor, the Tulsa station, gave notice of appeal. Because they had such tremendous resources compared to our relative poverty, they had a good chance of overturning the examiner's decision.

Our adversaries wanted to enjoin us from going on the air until they had time to show why they should have received the license. Mr. Kennedy realized there was one way he could defeat them. That was for us to quickly get on the air so the legal point would be moot.

He then pulled the biggest of surprises. His standard method of operation was to spend months and years in planning, designing and redesigning. None of us had ever seen him hurry or act spontaneously. Uncharacteristically, Mr. Kennedy sprinted.

In a burst of record-breaking speed, steelworkers were rushed to what we called "the farm." It was a plot of land in the middle of a field of milo on a dirt road, nearer to Robstown than to Corpus Christi. There, out of sight from anyone passing on the highway, a television tower arose. A contractor went to work building a small studio and control room.

No one mentioned this, even to one other. It was said that all the construction work was done in the dead of night. That probably was a metaphor. However, it was done with such secrecy that the station came into being as unexpectedly as a high-tech visual effect.

The control room was completely equipped and could send out audio and video signals. The only visuals were those on film. Tape had not yet come into use. No live pictures could be sent, because there were no cameras on the floor of the studio. The studio was devoid of any furnishing.

An orange crate with a microphone on it stood on one side of the room. Gene Looper stood in front of the mike. Mr. Kennedy and I flanked him.

The engineer threw a switch. Looper's deep, authoritative voice announced to the biosphere, "This is KSIX-TV signing on the air on Channel 10, September 30, 1956, and operating in the public interest." He delineated frequency and other technical information. Tears dripped down my face.

No one heard us, of course. We were probably the only television station in the world to sneak on the air, letting no one know that we existed. We had activated our license and were operating legally. What even we didn't know was that we had breathed life into an electronic monster that would devour our hours and energy for years to come.

21

Lights, Camera, Action

Stepping off into the unknown, we had pursued and captured a television channel. Now, we had to figure out what to do with the beast. Leaving the known behind, I saw all possibilities as an astronaut in years to come would see from a spaceship the earth ball in its entirety.

The first weeks we were on the air, the transmitter sent out a few hours of film and public service announcements, still incognito. Equipment, including floor cameras, arrived. An experienced camera crew was hired and came from Shreveport, Louisiana.

As far as my best friend, Marg Brown, and I were concerned, we were now ready to begin live telecasting. She didn't work for the station but was involved in whatever I did, as I was in what she did. Marg had worked briefly for a television station in San Francisco, so she was my expert. An election was coming up, with a number of civic issues on the ballot. Marg and I decided we'd have a production to keep viewers abreast of election returns.

Since there was nothing in the studio but two cameras, we brought furniture from our homes and created sets. We conned a radio salesman into selling packages of television commercials.

The Chamber of Commerce was strongly supporting certain issues on the ballot. We invited officers and directors of the Chamber to participate in the telecast as commentators. None of them had ever been in a television studio, and every one accepted our invitation with alacrity.

The most emotional issue on the ballot was whether or not the city would approve a dog leash law. Marg and I went to the city pound and selected a personality pooch.

Mr. Kennedy knew that we planned to telecast returns. He thought we would compile statistics, create graphics, and project them from the control room. Somehow, I failed to convey to him that we were staging what was now a full-blown gala in our pristine studio.

"You are going to do what?" he demanded, when he received the first hint.

Learning that Chamber directors would be guest stars, he mumbled in disbelief, "Prominent civic leaders will be there to watch this fiasco! You don't know what you are doing!"

A few more details were revealed. "Commercials have been sold. Marg Brown is going to type messages live, the camera showing her hands as the type appears."

Desperation was in his voice. "She'll make typos, and we'll look ridiculous!"

"There's one more thing," I told him. "We've borrowed a dog from the pound. If returns are coming in favoring the dog, I'll take his leash off. If the law is passing, I'll put the leash on."

There was no color left in Mr. K's rather ruddy complexion. Although a sturdy man, he appeared near collapse. Finally, he drew in enough breath to order, "There will be no dog in my studio!"

My job was obviously on the line. It didn't matter. I was addicted to television. Not too much later, I'd go through a slow, debilitating withdrawal, but right now this rarefied atmosphere of show biz was heady.

The telecast was carried off as though rehearsed and produced by competent people. Marg did not hit a wrong key on the typewriter. Chamber directors made enlightening statements about the future of the city as portended by the vote. The dog did not raise his leg to water any director's shoe. He was leashed.

No one saw the telecast, as far as I know. We had neither advertised nor promoted it. Almost no one knew the station was on the air. Few people had television sets in their homes. No matter. We had produced a live telecast, and to us it was a great triumph.

From Mr. Kennedy's rather more conservative evaluation, the

whole episode indicated one thing: I needed to be trained. My days on the road began.

My first course in continuing education was in Evanston, Illinois, at Northwestern University. These were the innocent days of television. I learned the ethics and high standards to which news directors—all men—pledged themselves. At that time, I was the only woman news director of a television-and-radio operation in the United States.

Those of us in the Northwestern class self-righteously took our pledge. News would never be sensationalized; it would be balanced fare, presented in depth. Commercials in newscasts would be in no way misrepresentative. There would be no contact between news and advertising in our stations.

Ratings would not influence news in any way. No advertiser would be allowed to use such words as "flash!" or "bulletin!" No advertiser could make his own pitch on camera, but the message would be transmitted by a dignified and professional announcer. Ha!

In Kansas City, I took a course in photography in a commercial laboratory. At the University of Oklahoma campus in Norman, I learned techniques of filming. Some of the nation's finest cameramen were gathered there for update sessions.

I learned how to theme every film I shot. Photographing a parade does not tell a story. Shoot the parade through the eyes of the widow of an old soldier sitting on the curb. Don't pan, blurring your picture with camera movement. Use sequence shots to move from place to place with a long shot, a medium shot, and a close-up.

I took almost word-for-word notes. The dean of cameramen, Joe Costa, once of the *New York World*, was one of the teachers. He was kind and considerate. I was the only person there who was not a professional cameraman and knew nothing. Joe adopted me as his friend.

When the session was over, he commissioned me to write an article, which he illustrated, for the *National Cameraman's Magazine*. Later, he visited me in Corpus Christi and explored the King Ranch, with Cecil Burney as his host.

Burney was one of the few Texas attorneys working with cameramen nationally to get permission for cameras in the courtroom under controlled conditions. Their idea was basically one pool-camera shooting unseen through a hole in the wall from an adjoining room. Listen up, O.J.!

Juliet with camera.

In between jaunts for training, I put together a seven-man news staff for KZTV, with Ken Cessna as night editor. None except Ken had any electronic news experience. I brought home to the staff what I was learning in my courses. Eventually, we had what I think was one of the best news teams that ever worked in a market of this size.

As always, I wanted to move faster than Mr. Kennedy would allow. Our first newscasts were only talking heads. We shot many pictures for radio, at a time before I knew we were going to use them in a television application. For television, we had no pictures. Gradually, we introduced photos, first Polaroid pictures, then eight-by-ten stills. Everything up to this time was in black and white. Color slides came next. Finally, we began shooting, editing, and projecting film.

I had little time for airwork. I did produce documentaries and narrate them, and occasionally I interviewed on the air someone of special interest. Most of my efforts were, with the staff, to write stories and compile newscasts with context that would give an in-depth understanding of what had happened that day.

We were forever designing our "cathedral studios," which Mr. K promised would be built. In truth, almost twenty years later one of the best thought-out facilities for television and radio that could be designed was constructed. Station managers come from a wide geographic area to tour the station and take away ideas to improve their own operations.

For years before the cathedral studios materialized, we worked in uptown offices, assembling newscasts that were driven twenty miles to "the farm." No computers, no fax, just typewritten stories with carbon copies and visuals.

Three commercial stations now had news staffs on the street and were competing with us. We won almost every category of news awards given in the state of Texas. Only once were we beaten in the ratings.

That was when KRIS-TV went "blood and guts." Their cameramen chased every ambulance and fire truck. Their newscasts were a montage of pain and death, much like television dramas today. At first their news stole away our viewers. Thirty minutes of wrecks, stabbing, shootings, drownings, and fires burned itself out after a few months, and we got our audience back.

Television stations did not have meteorologists in the fifties. We had announcers who knew nothing of the vagaries of coastal weather. We received continual teletype data from the local weather station, but it was almost useless. The national Weather Bureau at that time sent all forecasts from New Orleans to the Corpus Christi weather station at the airport.

The airport station was allowed to pass on to us only what New Orleans said. If New Orleans said the sun was shining in Corpus Christi and the temperature was ninety degrees, that was what we were advised by teletype. This was despite the fact that an employee at the airport could look out and see pouring rain and a thermometer registering seventy degrees.

As long as no weather extremes threatened, we could work around these minor irritations. If there was a hurricane out there or some other threat to life and property, something more had to be done.

I learned that the navy had excellent meteorologists, but they were not allowed to give information to newsmen or the general public in competition with the Weather Bureau. They could, though, within their restrictions, provide the mayor of the city with answers to any questions he asked.

I worked out a deal with whomever was mayor at the time. When it was urgent for his constituents to receive the most accurate predictions possible in the technology of that era, he would call the navy, get the information I wanted, and pass it on to me. My weather casts frequently quoted the mayor.

This was another of those circumstances that caused Mr. Kennedy to call me in for interrogation. "Why are we quoting the mayor instead of the Weather Bureau as our authority?"

I explained the situation.

As it turned out, some of the best television news that Corpus Christi would ever see was produced in those first years. None of our viewers knew how television news should be presented. As amateurs, we didn't hesitate to experiment, since we had few preconceived ideas. We had the best production staff that the station would ever have.

Truly, we were pioneers in South Texas, willing to enter unfamiliar territory and take risks. We had faith and leapt from heights. We had to be taught to fear ratings and the bottom line.

22

A Genius and a Gentleman

Vann M. Kennedy was one of a number of people, beginning with my father, who accepted me as I was but continually introduced to me new ideas that I could explore and accept if I wished. This, to me, is education.

To Mr. Kennedy, the written word is the fundamental stepping stone to communication, an essential of civilization. Each year, he gives thousands of books to close friends and momentary acquaintances. Yet it was in verbal communication that he invested his total monetary worth to establish a radio station that would become the cornerstone of a multimillion-dollar South Texas electronic holding.

Incongruities like that made it impossible for those of us who worked for him to ever presume to predict Mr. K's moves. All we were sure of was that whatever he had chosen to be, he would have been the best.

I believe he chose his career because there were two aspects of his being that dominated: the value that he placed on accurate and informative news, and the compulsion of entrepreneurship.

We shared the passionate belief that reporting important news

Juliet, Vann Kennedy, and KSIX announcer.

in a comprehensive way was imperative if our form of government was to survive. In other respects, no two people could be more different than we were.

Mr. Kennedy was a scholar. Before he made a decision or took any action, he read everything available on the subject. He talked to the people most knowledgeable in the field, wherever they were and whatever their positions. Then he filtered all the information he had accumulated through the fine screen of his mind. Whatever the outcome, he let time pass to make sure he had reached the best conclusion.

I, on the other hand, reacted spontaneously, going into action immediately, learning what I could on the run, and reaching the stage of accomplished fact in hardly any time at all.

His demeanor was always formal. I was casual to an extreme. Late one night, when some story was breaking and I was still on the job after working twelve or fourteen hours, I needed to confer with him on some detail. Forgetting that I had taken off my shoes, I dashed into Mr. K's office barefooted.

I interrupted what he was doing, asking, "Do you have time to talk to me?"

He got up slowly from his chair, bowed, and said in his favorite drawl, "I always have time for a gracious lady."

It is a dichotomy that my respect for him was boundless, yet we were combative, usually in the politest of ways, but not always. Sometimes, my insubordination brought a dangerous glint of contained violence to his eyes.

I was an idealist, and in ways he was, too. The difference was that I had no interest in the business office. He knew his first responsibility was to keep us afloat financially, or we couldn't attain any of the things that we both wanted to do.

One issue we debated year in, year out, was benefits for employees, including health insurance and higher salaries. Mr. Kennedy was satisfied with bringing in young people, giving them a chance, training them, then letting them rise to the top in bigger markets. I wanted to keep some of that talent after we developed it.

A feeling we shared was love for his daughter, Kathleen. She was three years old when I first saw her, much like her father, blond, intelligent, rational. Chris Wenger taught her to sail in a boat we owned named *Egret*. We spent many happy hours on the water.

Later she would enroll in sailing program offered in England and in which she moved up to the top of the ranks.

Her first interest was marine science. When she reached college age, Mr. K agreed to her choice of a study of science but said her first degree should be in journalism. He foresaw the area of communication and information when the great need would be for articulate scientists who could help people at all levels of education understand new technology.

Kathleen eventually received a Ph.D. in microbiology and did post-doctoral work with Nobel Prize winners in Switzerland. She has taken advantage of her journalistic and scientific background by working in both research and education and applying it to business and economics.

Mary Kennedy and I visited her in Basel, and we all traveled together aross the Alps and to Vienna. We have seldom gotten to sail together in later years, but she has sailed many waters.

When applying for our television license, I dug into Mr. K's background to write the exhibits we submitted to the FCC.

He was born in Alabama about the same time that his father, a physician, died of tuberculosis. His mother brought the family to Texas, where she was able to find work to support her son and a daughter.

From childhood, the young Kennedy held what jobs he could find, sweeping out businesses, delivering milk and newspapers. At sixteen, he built a radio receiver out of a coil of wire, a crystal detector, and an oatmeal box.

During his years in college and law school, he worked as a newspaper circulation director and on the side installed those "newfangled" radios in private homes. From there, he moved into the job of police reporter and on to the courthouse beat for the *San Antonio Express*.

At law school in Austin, he was a stringer for the state's leading newspapers. He used what money he had saved to found the *Capital Weekly Press*. He passed the bar exam and went to work as bureau chief in Austin for International News Service.

It was there that he hired a cub reporter named Walter Cronkite and trained him for a year, until Cronkite went on to a Houston newspaper, eventually becoming the nation's most admired news commentator.

A Genius and a Gentleman 101

Mr. Kennedy and Cronkite remained close friends. I met Cronkite on several occasions. He calls Mr. K his mentor and told me that he learned more from Kennedy than from all his years in college. I accused Cronkite of stealing that line from me, as I have said the same thing so many times.

In Austin, Mr. K met his future wife, Mary Whittleff. She had left Cleveland, Ohio, to further a career in journalism. During World War II, Mr. K, with the rank of colonel, served in China and India and was decorated by both the United States and the Republic of China.

During a tour of duty in Washington, the WACs (Women's Army Corps) were under his command, and he worked with Oveta Culp Hobby, who was director of the WACs, a cabinet officer, and editor and president of the *Houston Post*.

While Mr. Kennedy was at war, Mary managed his Austin businesses, which included an oil-and-gas magazine that he founded, *The State Observer*, and a print shop that handled nine publications. It became impossible to find staff for the businesses. Mary sold the *Observer* and the press, each for $5,000. When "Colonel" Kennedy returned to civilian life, he added $5,000 in termination pay to the money she had made, and with that stake they established a radio station in Corpus Christi. Involved in the business were several men with whom he had served, including attorney Cecil Burney, my good friend from college days.

I went to work for Mr. Kennedy three years later. During the time I worked for him, we obtained licenses and put television stations on the air in Corpus Christi and Laredo.

He was an important figure in the conservative wing of the Democratic Party of Texas. Officeholders and candidates called upon him in great number, seeking his advice, which was highly respected.

I would sit and listen intently when I was in his office and he received telephone calls from President Lyndon Johnson or House Speaker Sam Rayburn. Some of the most prominent men in the nation nurtured friendships with "Vann." His employees never called him by his first name, not even me, someone who seldom remembers anyone's last name.

He was an extremely patriotic man. He was equally modest and shy. Never did he allow any such word as "rape" to go on the air. I was instructed to say criminal assault.

One morning, I learned that a prominent citizen of Corpus Christi had been shot and killed in the border town of Matamoros, Mexico. I called International News Service to get the story for me. It moved while the noon newscast was on the air, so that I had no time to do anything but tear it off the machine and take it to the announcer to read.

After the newscast, I was called into Mr. Kennedy's office and greeted with the words, "I hope you can prove that!"

"Prove what?" I asked him.

"That the gentleman was shot in a bordello."

"No," I said, "I don't know the names of the subdivisions in Matamoros."

"A bordello," he almost hissed at me, "is a house of ill repute."

I hadn't known that. The rest of the day, Mr. K came in and out of my office saying various obscene words and asking me if I knew their meanings. It must have been extremely difficult for him, as it was deeply instilled in him that such words should not be heard by a lady. Nevertheless, as an attorney and station owner, he had to try to protect us from libel by naiveté.

Another time, I again heard him say, "Can you prove that?!" Police Captain Louie Davis had called me. He named a club on North Beach and said, "We raided it last night and made gambling arrests. The club owner said, 'You can't do this. Chief Roy Lay told me the heat was off, and we could open up again.'" Louie paused, then said, "What do you think of that?"

I replied, "I think it is a heck of a good story. May I quote you?"

I expected him to scream, "Of course not!" Instead he said, "I don't see why not. It's the truth."

That was enough for me. I aired it.

Mr. K instructed me to follow up the news angles, investigate, and put together a case so that we could defend ourselves if we were sued.

Louie called me back a few minutes later. "The chief's mad as hell," he said. "Would you believe that?"

I certainly would. The chief tried everything he could think of to get me barred from the police station but didn't succeed. After an investigation by internal affairs, he was demoted and a new chief named.

Mr. Kennedy never interfered with my operation of the news bureau or suggested what stories I should or should not use. However, he never stopped teaching me. Every day for several years after I went to work for him, I went into his office after each news broadcast and we went over the stories together.

In a conversational way, without finding fault, we discussed where a word could be more precise, where I could have used a more appealing word, such as "home" instead of "house," how I could have clarified a situation to answer more of the questions viewers might have, or where I could look for a follow-up that my competitors might overlook to give myself an exclusive.

Mr. Kennedy usually wore a white linen suit, which made him look like a plantation owner. His slow, considered approach to all things lent him great dignity. Somewhere under that impressive exterior, there must have been a would-be irresponsible kid who loved to get a beat on a story and shake up the town. Otherwise, he would have fired me at least once a week for twenty-one years. Bless him, he never did.

23
Only the Best

After much dedication, hard work, and a little trial and error, the staff of the KZTV news bureau synthesized into a miniature universe. Each member offered a different ingredient to its integrity.

We were in a small television market where pay was too low to attract established newsmen to the staff. Instead, I looked for intelligent, creative people with intellectual curiosity who enjoyed learning.

Every morning, I assigned stories that could be scheduled. Ken Cessna, the night editor, made his own rounds, contributed to earlier newscasts, and then took over to put out the ten o'clock news and sports. All the reporters doubled as cameramen.

After the staff had sufficient experience working together, administration occupied the smallest percentage of my time, and I had more time to gather and write news. That's the thing I live to do. Every story I work is like living a mini-life to me and lets me identify a little more of where I fit into the whole of things.

When I was not working a story on the street, I was at my desk with a police scanner behind me, taking stories by telephone and writing them. We were on top of breaking stories, both from the scanner and from good contacts who called us quickly after an event occurred.

Only the Best 105

We might write as many as thirty short stories for the noon broadcast. By 4:00 in the afternoon, the reporters turned in their stories and graphics, which I worked in with my stories. We all wrote the newscasts for the radio announcers and for the two television anchormen, Gene Looper and Walter Furley.

As a rule, the anchor drove the news package to the studio which, with the transmitting tower, was almost twenty miles away. If for some reason either Looper or Furley was already at the farm, a substitute handled the messenger service. This was a dangerous business, rushing the newscast from one facility to the other in heavy traffic and all kinds of weather. On one trip, Gene Looper was involved in a terrible automobile accident and broke his back. A trouper, he did not take much time off before he returned to the job in a body cast. Soon enough, there came a time when his back didn't hurt so much as it itched. I bought him a long wooden back scratcher, which he says certified friendship for a lifetime.

Another disaster occurred late one Saturday night as reporter Leigh Anthony was making the run. Rain was coming down in torrents, and when he turned off the highway onto the country road that led to the transmitter, his car stalled out. Leigh got out of the car and began wading through mud. Before he arrived at his destination, he had to crawl part of the way. The paper on which the newscast was written was sopping wet and muddy by the time he made his dramatic appearance in the studio. The newscast was almost impossible to read, but Looper, an amateur magician by avocation and a smoothie when it comes to ad-libbing, told our listeners something or other that night. There is no record of exactly what.

In the newsroom, the cast of characters was versatile. Two anchors whose voices made the news compelling, Walter Furley and Gene Looper, contributed greatly to the news team in many ways. One unusual thing about Furley and Looper is that each has remained at the station for over fifty years, Gene as program director and Walter now as news director.

Cessna, the night editor, became a well-known news personality as he did some work on camera and extensive sportscasting. He was the staff's stability—always predictable and dependable. He built a loyal following of news contacts, especially at the courthouse, who saw to it that he was the first to know whatever was happening. He arrived on time each day, left at noon for a game of dominoes in the sandwich shop during the lunch hour, and at quitting time, whether or not a UFO was hanging over the city, his golf clubs were in the passenger seat of his MG convertible and he was on his way to the first tee.

Among the reporters, Bob Odom was the quiet one whose methodical mind put everything in order. He could walk into any situation, deal with it capably, and come out with a complete and well-balanced story. When he first started working in television, he had never held any camera more complicated than a Kodak Brownie. Sequestering himself with operators' manuals, he learned within a short time how to take apart any camera in the place, put it back together, load it, and shoot well-composed pictures. He was to become editor and then publisher of the *Kingsville Record News*.

Reporter Larry Ray was truly an excellent writer and photographer. My mistake was to assign him to interview the head of American Red Cross when that dignitary was in town. Before Larry returned to the office, he had been offered and had accepted a position as head of Red Cross in Japan.

Another of our excellent reporters, Don Tooker, had extraordinarily deep convictions about how human beings should treat one other. He did not grind out one story after another. He polished each as though it were a flawless piece of jade. A sculptor of jade was actually the subject of one of his most beautiful film stories.

Leigh Anthony was someone on our team who never ceased to amaze me. He had an encyclopedic mind. There was no need to open a reference book when he was around. He could answer any question I had. I assigned him to interview an Orthodox Greek prelate who was touring this country. Much to the prelate's amazement and mine, Anthony interviewed him in Greek.

Nicknamed "Thunder," reporter Girard Thornton was a tall young man who went into action with the velocity of a body thrown from a motorcycle in a collision. He couldn't pass a single piece of furniture without bruising himself and never failed to stumble over any obstacle. He was always on the starting line, carrying cameras, strobe lights, and other odds and ends of hardware on straps over his shoulder.

One afternoon, a dispatcher's voice on a police scanner advised us that a robbery was underway at a nearby bank. "Go!" I

Only the Best 107

said. Thunder took flight. He arrived at the bank at the same time police did. Everybody was running in, apprehensive, unsure whether armed robbers were still on the scene. Thunder tripped and fell headlong, all of his equipment clattering loudly as it bounded along the floor. Reflex action brought every policeman to killer stance with handguns drawn. Thunder later became a Protestant minister.

Richard Tillery was a member of our group who was usually something of a cynic but whose heart could still be touched. He covered the story when a Reynolds Metals ship picked up survivors about to drown in the Gulf of Mexico after attempting to escape Cuba in small boats. They were brought into the Reynolds plant in San Patricio County and stayed in South Texas. Tillery kept in touch with them in the months that followed, making sure these refugee families had shelter, work, and other needs met.

After the devastation of Hurricane Celia, he was one of the first persons ashore on Mustang Island, where he found the mayor of Port Aransas using the city's large generator to keep his beer cold. Richard asked pointed questions, and the mayor called the island constabulary and had him thrown in jail.

Any technician can write an acceptable story about sensational breaking news or an illustrious person. The exceptional writer is the one who can take what others see as commonplace and derive from it a compelling story. This was Jack Galloway.

Jack could go to a Junior League rummage sale and return with a lyrical narrative and a film of memorable delicacy. Sadly, he had such sensitivity to others that the realities of general news were hurtful to him personally.

One afternoon, he covered a story in a Robstown barrio involving a family living in subhuman circumstances. He didn't come back. That barrio was not a totally safe place to be, so I finally called his home. He answered, telling me, "I was too depressed to come back to work. I hope you understand, but if you don't, you don't."

At the police station one day, he talked to a runaway child, a small boy who was considered to be a liar because he had made up a life story. In his own mind, the boy was creating an alternative life for himself. Reality was more than he could accept. The boy had been burned with cigarettes, beaten with red-hot coathangers, and otherwise tortured. Child Protective Services took him into custody. Jack and his wife, who had two children, offered to adopt the abused child if courts severed parental rights. They did not. A judge gave the child back to his abusing parents, saying that under all circumstances, children were better off with birth parents, and parents had a right to discipline their children in their own way.

Jack became a professional photographer, shooting a great deal of art photography, and authored a sensitive novel about the relationship of a boy and his kidnapper, *The Toothache Tree*.

What everyone on the staff at KZTV had in common was the ability to recognize news and communicate it in a way distinctly his own. We were not a family. We were not buddies. We were individuals who had a common goal and achieved it by respecting one another and cooperating.

24
Delinquent Parents

Whenever I get to know a child characterized as a juvenile delinquent, I try to figure out what changes it would have made in me if I had been reared in the circumstances he or she experienced. For KZTV newscasts, the police allowed me to write the stories of these children as long as I did not identify them on air.

One child I will never forget is Dennie Betts. Dennie was in the juvenile shelter frequently, picked up as a habitual runaway. He ran away whenever he thought his drunken stepfather was going to beat him to death. He slept in high weeds in vacant lots, and in daylight he searched for food until he was spotted and taken back to the shelter.

One day when he was leaving the shelter, he managed to get my address. He showed up at my front door. He wanted to attend a scout camp. He said if I would lend him the money, he would pay me back with yard work. Instinctively, I trusted him. He lived up to his word and worked for me diligently. He was a bright, inquisitive child who learned rapidly.

One night I was in the news bureau when I heard a call put out over the police radio for detectives to come to the scene of a murder. I drove to the address given. When I got out of the car, a child ran toward me through the darkness and threw his arms around me. It was Dennie.

"He murdered my mother," the boy wept, digging his face into my chest.

The stepfather, abusive to both his wife and stepson, had done what Dennie had feared most. There were two small children in the house, Dennie's half-brother and half-sister. A neighbor, who was the little girl's teacher, took her home. I took Dennie and his little brother to my house.

We put the small boy to bed, then Dennie called his mother's parents in Illinois. They said they would send money for me to put the three children on a plane to come live with them in a house in the country.

The next day, we took care of all the necessary tasks that we could. I learned to my dismay that the stepfather had been released on bail. Then I found out he was looking for the children.

I called District Judge Paul Martineau, for whom the juvenile shelter was named, and told him I was going to keep the children hidden until I could get them on a plane. I did not want to be charged with kidnapping. He said, "I don't want to know any details. Protect the children. I'll protect you if necessary."

I took the three children to the Municipal Coliseum, where my friend Marg Brown was manager, a place where I did not think the father would look for them. I left them there under her care while I went to see the airline manager, tell him the story, and get tickets and his cooperation. He alerted a pilot and stewardess that I would be arriving with the children immediately before the plane took off.

Near departure time, I put the three of them in my car and drove around on back roads near the airport. At the last minute, I drove into the terminal area and with the children ran for the plane. The stewardess closed the door behind them, and the plane began taxiing immediately.

They made it to Illinois and the home of the grandparents. Unfortunately, a judge in Illinois issued an order requiring the grandparents to turn the two younger children over to their father, and he took them away. The little girl died quite young. Her brother survived.

Dennie was happy living on the farm, even though he felt con-

Delinquent Parents 111

cern for the other two children. He completed his high-school education, did well-paid shift work, saved money, and established his own business. He married and had children of his own, and he brought his family to Texas to see me. He did mention from time to time that he and his wife were making sure their children had love, attention, and measured discipline. We exchange e-mails. He has a successful antiques business and recently has been selling on the Internet.

Examining Dennie's life and thinking of mine, several things came to mind. When I was Dennie's age, in my early teens, no one used the word "delinquents." When we stepped past the boundaries established for the conduct of truthful and obedient children, our actions were described as childish escapades.

One "escapade" that I remember pulling during those years was repeated more than once. The family of James P. and Mabel Luby lived right behind my family in the Del Mar subdivision in Corpus Christi in winter when the children were in school. I was an only child, and the Lubys had nine surviving children. Where they went, I went. Mrs. Luby did not notice one more child.

The Lubys had large ranch holdings. Their grandfather, Judge James O. Luby, a patriarch in Duval County, sat on the bench at a time when a judge was omnipotent, doing justice as he saw it in cases involving land and water rights, fence lines, and cattle brands. He would tell me about the Battle of Shiloh and the fight at Palmetto Rancho.

I had to pull every scam I could think of to keep my mother in Corpus Christi from learning details of my life at the ranch headquarters, which was a large house with the Jim Wells and Duval County lines running through the middle of it. George Parr, "the Duke of Duval," taught me to roll my own cigarettes at the quarterhorse racetrack, where Anna Maria Luby, called "Tootie," and I went as often as possible.

Tootie and I would sometimes talk the mail carrier into letting us ride in his car with chains that skidded down muddy ruts to Freer. The oil boom was underway. Fistfights at saloons were too frequent for us to stop and watch long. We were impressed by a high noon shootout we watched from a shop doorway.

We'd sneak out of the house at night. If someone had died that day, we'd stop at his home and listen to the shrieks and moans of the professional mourners. Then we'd go either to Rancho Grande or Casa Blanca, nightclubs with casinos as open as those at Vegas today. I was lucky at blackjack. When I had a winning streak, cowboys would drop big bills on my quarter bets. These were Depression times. I don't know where we got the quarters to bet. Prohibition was still in effect. Nobody worried about the fact that Tootie and I were underage, or that gambling and serving mixed drinks were against the law.

Sometimes there'd be a raid. Law-enforcement officers would walk in wearing side arms, confiscate all the money in sight, go to the bar, order drinks all around, and divvy up the money. This was the free state of Duval. When I returned to my own home in Corpus Christi, I reverted in large degree to being the proper child. I could have been picked up as a delinquent in San Diego, except most of us wouldn't have known what the word meant.

25

Embattled Empire

One of the longest-running news stories in Texas in the latter half of this century had all the elements of a suspense thriller. Set in the expanses of perhaps the worlds largest oil-rich ranch, its main characters included Sarita Kenedy East, a lonely, remote philanthropist; and Brother Leo, a monk who would later become a complete hermit. Even the Pope at the Vatican played a cameo role. I covered the story on KZTV newscasts from its beginning to its end.

Unpredictably, this story changed my life, because the monk involved got me in touch with my own spirituality.

The news story broke after Sarita died of cancer in 1961. In her will she left the Kenedy Ranch and all its surface and subsurface resources to "the poorest of the poor." That had been her greatest desire, to better the life of some of those who had the least in this world. To carry out the mandates of her will, she named three executors, one of them Brother Leo.

The ranch itself is a huge acreage of Texas lore. It came into being after the War Between the States. Mifflin Kenedy, a riverboat captain who had fought for the South, established a ranch with his partner, Richard King. The two spreads were later divided.

The Kings bred cattle and racehorses, conducted ranch research, entertained royalty, and were among the nation's most fabled families. The Kenedys lived quietly, a private family, providing well for their ranch hands, immersed in their religion.

Sarita was the last of the direct heirs, a romantic, shadowy figure. She lived alone in a Spanish-style home some distance from the ranch headquarters, in a small town named for her.

I knew Sarita when I was a child. One of my friends, Connie Glazebrook, lived in what is now Centennial House on Corpus Christi's Bluff. Her father was manager of the Kenedy Ranch and had an apartment in the village of Sarita. The community is the Kenedy County seat and is unique in that it is the only county seat in Texas that can be entered only by crossing a cattleguard.

Connie and I would spend weekends with her family in the apartment there. Sarita's cousins, the East brothers, were about our age. They took Connie and me horseback riding on the ranch, across miles of brush country and cactus to the shores of the Gulf of Mexico.

We were in and out of the ranch house. Sarita was always pleasant to us but rather formal. She could have been a character out of a Brontë novel. Alone in unpopulated brush country, her attire was that of the proper Victorian woman, a dark dress, tight bodice, full skirt, and white lace collar.

Some years later, Sarita made a bequest of a million dollars to the Roman Catholic Diocese of Corpus Christi, with the provision that it be spent on the poorest of the poor. No direct connection was established, but a mansion on a large Ocean Drive property in Corpus Christi was acquired by the church as the Bishop's Palace.

Sarita had written a will in which the Diocese of Corpus Christi was the recipient of the greatest largess. She changed her will.

On the East Coast, an order of cloistered monks had financial needs. They sent Brother Leo, one of their own, away from the life of silence and meditation to appeal for assistance from the ranch woman. He became Sarita's spiritual advisor. Rumor had it that in her secluded existence she had abused alcohol and that the monk helped her make changes in her life.

She and Brother Leo went to Chile, to a highly impoverished part of that country. She bought a large block of land and initiated a project to build comfortable and affordable housing for people in extreme poverty. For a time, she and Brother Leo carried out much that she had expressed a desire to do.

Embattled Empire 115

Sarita's life ended. The court case began. The bishop of the diocese, a bank, and several of Sarita's relatives sued to break the will. Contenders for the estate alleged that Brother Leo had used undue influence on Sarita.

Weeks, months, and years passed as exhibits and evidence piled up, filling law offices and court storage areas. The legal complexities of the case were reported by newspapers and television. Hearsay was often more interesting.

From Rome came the backing of the Pope for the bishop. Brother Leo's order did not defrock him but did not allow him to return to the cloister, because he was not being obedient to the church hierarchy.

He had no money. He was supported by a number of wealthy South Texans who had been Sarita's friends. Respected and highly paid attorneys donated their services to represent him.

From time to time, rulings were handed down on issues in the case. In each instance, the bishop was the winner, as he was in a final judgment. Appeals began, but the money, amounting to millions of dollars a year, by order of the court now went to a foundation that the court set up with a board chaired by the bishop.

One of the most conspicuous results of the new wealth of the diocese was establishment of a radio and television station. The radio studios were more lavish than those from which networks broadcast in New York or Los Angeles.

As I tracked the story for more than twenty years, I became engrossed in the person of the monk. He had chosen to live a life of poverty and contemplation, yet stood his ground against all to whom he had voluntarily been subservient.

One of his attorneys was Frances Farenthold, the daughter of Dudley Tarleton, a Corpus Christi attorney known for his masterful oratory. She was the second wife of George Farenthold, a Belgian baron who came to this country to marry a wealthy Corpus Christi woman.

After she raised a family, Frances became a political activist, a state representative, and a devout feminist. I asked her one day, "What kind of a person is Brother Leo? Is he a saint or a devil? From all the strong feelings I have heard expressed about him, I am convinced he has to be one or the other."

Frances laughed at my question but didn't answer it. Not long after that, she called me at the television newsroom one morning and said, "Meet me for lunch at the little German restaurant on Leopard Street."

I did. She walked in with a tall man wearing black slacks, a white shirt and tennis shoes. "There he is," she said. "Decide for yourself."

Brother Leo and I sat down and started talking. We've never stopped communicating: in conversation, by mail, and now by e-mail.

One of the first questions I asked him was, "How do you have the fortitude to go on fighting year after year against one of the wealthiest and most powerful institutions in the world when you never win a single skirmish?"

He smiled at me. "Sarita put her trust in me. As long as I live, I'll do everything that I can to carry out her commission."

"Are you never discouraged?"

"No. I do what my inner voice tells me. I cannot control the results. That is in God's hands."

I found a faith in Brother Leo exceeding that which I have known in any other mortal. He accepts the world as it is, as God's creation. That includes me, cradle Episcopalian that I am. He is totally nonjudgmental. At the same time, he speaks the truth as he perceives it, which may be articulated in harsh words.

His love of each person as a child of God comes across with such tenderness that sometimes it brings tears to my eyes. His strength is in his submission to what he believes to be God's will.

Probably what he has told me most often is "Ask for nothing except that God's will be done."

My inclination as a person was to accept everything he told me about the Kenedy Ranch case as incontrovertible. As a reporter, I had to verify or disprove everything he said by any possible source.

Major Tom Armstrong, a part of the King Ranch family and a close friend of Sarita's, was still alive then. I called him and asked him what he knew to be fact, what he had been told by Sarita herself. He confirmed all that Brother Leo had said.

He also told me that the late Henrietta Kleberg, another member of the King Ranch family and Sarita's confidant, had discussed the subjects in-depth with him before she died. Henrietta was convinced that Sarita was rational and acting of her own free will when she decided what disposition she wanted made of her estate.

Another of Sarita's close friends was Wash Storm, a nurseryman and judge in Jim Wells County. I had covered cases in his court and had gotten to know and respect him as a dispassionate judge and a man of integrity. He related conversations he had had with Sarita that left no doubt in his mind about her intentions and motivation.

The appeals process dragged on. Brother Leo's presence was no longer required in Texas. He went to mountains on the island of Martinique. There he lived as a hermit in a lean-to by the side of a stream, a two-day walk to a village where he bought supplies and received mail.

He wrote me long letters, quoting from scripture or from the writings of great thinkers, whether they be Catholic, Protestant, Jewish, Hindu, or agnostic. Among the figures of history he most admired was Mahatma Gandhi, whose nonviolent persistence changed at least a part of the world.

Brother Leo reminds me in almost every letter to quiet my mind so that I can hear my inner voice. He quotes scriptures that warn against listening for truth in thunder or the babble of tongues.

Periodically, he returns to Corpus Christi. Each time, we spend an afternoon drinking coffee at the Lighthouse Restaurant on the T-head, where we can watch boats come and go as we talk.

He has a sense of humor, and we laugh a lot, but most often he is serious.

"Don't let yourself be distracted from what you really want to do," he suggests. "Climb up on a plateau. From there, look down on all that is happening. Feel for the people there. Care what happens to them. Don't let yourself be emotionally involved in their conflicts or try to change their actions. Look within yourself to find what needs your attention and needs to be changed."

From Martinique, Brother Leo went to Argentina, where he lived in a solitary way, reading, thinking, meditating, spending much time in intercessory prayer. He rode a motorcycle when he needed to get around.

A *Wall Street Journal* writer, George Getschow, did extensive research and wrote a series of articles on the Kenedy Ranch court case in the *Journal*. He found much the same evidence that I had found to support all that Brother Leo said. George is now writing a book on the subject.

The appeals ended. The status of Sarita's estate still made

news. The Texas attorney general investigated allegations that the bishop, as chairman of the foundation committee, had not conformed to the courts' mandate in distributing the Kenedy Ranch money. Changes were made in the handling of the estate by the Foundation Board.

Finally, the story had an ending. The Holy See exonerated Brother Leo in 1997 by reinstating him in his order. A national magazine published by the Roman Catholic Church carried the story of the action taken in Rome relating to Brother Leo. The papers were delivered, as was the custom, to each church in the Diocese of Corpus Christi. Before members of the churches could pick up copies and read the story, all the papers in the diocese disappeared.

Brother Leo currently lives in Chile. During all the years of the court battle, he quietly sold off, a parcel at a time, property that Sarita had bought in his name. He used the money from each sale to build affordable housing for the poorest of the poor. The last piece of land that Sarita bought has been sold, but Brother Leo has found someone in Chile who is ready and able to carry on in Sarita's name, so more housing will still be built. Also during these years, Brother Leo founded new monasteries in Chile and may enter one of them when he completes the housing projects. We keep in touch with e-mail which he went into a nunnery to learn.

The literally billions of oil dollars that spew out of the Kenedy Ranch land have been given by the courts to the bishops. When Brother Leo speaks of the bishops, he says in an affectionate way, "I think they are embarrassed at times, God love 'em."

26

The Beltway

In addition to covering local news, I made several working trips to Washington to cover State Department briefings and major stories. I found it exhilarating to be where history had been and was being made. I relished covering stories with syndicated columnists whose writing I read daily and with correspondents I listened to nightly back home.

Washington has for me, a political junkie, some of the glitter that Hollywood has for movie fans. I feel pride as I walk down its streets. My thoughts move back to the days of my early history lessons, when I was taught that public officials of stature designed and carried out the art of government. Today, the consensus is that the land within "the Beltway" is a foreign country where a new species of people believes in totally different truths than those accepted in the United States.

I had an extraordinary guide, Sarah McClendon, the Texas newspaper correspondent who has been the bane of many a president. She was a close friend of Vann Kennedy, our station owner, who introduced me to her. With her, I moved at a fast clip from one legislative or executive office to another, to be in on anything newsworthy that was happening.

In briefings, information was often "background." I could

report whatever was said, but could not attribute it. When the briefings were over and I accompanied Sarah, everything was on the record.

As we walked through congressional halls, people appeared as though out of the walls, hailing Sarah down and giving her leads to important news stories or political gossip. Within a short time, she was able to contact the news sources involved for confirmation or denial of the tips.

On another trip, she called Pierre Salinger from her apartment, telling him in her most beguiling voice that she was bringing me to President John Kennedy's news conference that afternoon. He protested that I was not cleared by security and did not have credentials.

"You won't have trouble getting clearance for her. There's a dear. You always know how to do things no one else could accomplish. We'll pick up the credentials on our way in."

The credentials were waiting for us when we arrived. We were seated near correspondent Helen Thomas when she asked the first question. To me, the attitudes of the national correspondents and TV anchors were as interesting as their questions and the president's agility in answering them and in sparring with Sarah.

Civility still existed in Washington at that time. However, there was a difference in how reporters related to newsmakers in the nation's capital and in local city halls and courthouses. The questions we asked of our lawmakers in smaller cities were intended to solicit information. Only in instances where some wrongdoing was suspected did we probe in voices indicating we thought each answer was a lie. In Washington, questions and answers were part of a game in which bluffing was more important than the cards held.

A "photo op" gave me a chance to use my new credentials again. President Kennedy and Nikita Khrushchev were conferring in the Oval Office. I was ushered in with a small group of photographers. We stood quietly, getting our shots, as the two heads of state relaxed in comfortable chairs, conversing through interpreters. This was in 1963, when the United States and the Soviet Union agreed to run a hotline from the White House to the Kremlin.

On another trip, two other Texans and I were invited to The Elms for tea. The Elms had been the home of Pearl Metzger, known as "the hostess with the mostest," but Lyndon and Lady Bird Johnson and their daughters were living there at the time.

As I walked into The Elms, I passed Bobby Baker going out. He was notorious for questionable operations in which Johnson was suspected of being involved. Accusations ranged from undue influence of special interests to white-slavery rings. Nothing was ever proven. There were far fewer congressional investigations of the executive branch then.

Lady Bird Johnson served us tea in her friendly way. The vice-president sat in a rocking chair with one of his nearly grown daughters on his lap. We talked about everything from Texas wildflowers to operation of television stations. It was as informal as neighbors dropping in at home to drink coffee and chat.

I said nothing to remind Johnson that I had known him slightly when he was Congressman Dick Kleberg's secretary. I was in college at the time, and Mother had rented out my bedroom at home to help pay my bills.

Johnson rented the room for his younger brother, Sam, who had a drinking problem. Sam stayed in my room for two months. My mother was much too genteel to mention overdue rent. Sam's brother Lyndon came to see him late one night, and the next morning both Sam and his belongings were gone. So much for revenue for college.

After Lyndon became president, I would be a guest of the Johnsons again, at their Texas ranch. I attended a barbecue given in honor of the visiting president of Mexico.

All of us who were covering the event were driven around on a bus by a ranch hand who gave a running commentary. As we passed a slough, the driver pointed to a collection of small houses and said, "That's where the wetbacks and niggers live." Not a single reporter quoted that remark, which today would make headlines and cause riots. That is indicative of the difference in news coverage then and now.

27
Setting Sail

I went out with a photographer to shoot a feature on two young men from the Netherlands who had come to Corpus Christi and opened a factory to build thirteen-foot day-sailers called "Flying Dutchman Juniors." Their father, in Holland, had designed a popular class of boats, the "Flying Dutchman." This interview was nothing that I would expect to be pivotal in my life.

My friend Marg Brown was with me on the assignment. While I interviewed, and worked with the cameraman, Marg studied the various little fiberglass crafts on display.

When I finished my business, she said, "Since we live in a waterfront town, don't you think we should own a sailboat? Look at this one." She pointed to one with a turquoise hull. "Isn't it cute?"

We conferred, agreed, then called to one of the men I had been interviewing. "We want to buy a boat. We'll take the turquoise one."

The man, who spoke limited English, thought he had misunderstood. We convinced him that we were serious with a check, and he reluctantly agreed to launch the boat for us the next afternoon.

Driving back to work, Marg started having misgivings. "Do you know how to sail a boat?"

"Sure," I told her. "Nothing to it. When I was in high school, I sailed with my neighbor, Buddy Schwartz."

"It's not dangerous?" she asked.

With baseless bravado, I started telling her my sea tales. "One day we took a visiting inlander sailing. He was nervous, so Buddy couldn't resist tormenting him a bit. A gust of wind hit us at the wrong moment, and the boat heeled over with the lee rail in the water.

"The boat capsized. We didn't have life jackets, but we could all swim. I stood on the centerboard to right the boat, slipped, and the board's cutting edge ripped my leg above the knee. When we got the boat oriented and had climbed back in, the water was red with my blood sloshing around the bilge."

I don't know why I thought this horror story would reassure Marg. She asked, "Were you badly hurt?"

"Not really. Buddy sailed the boat to Cap Anderson's dock. No seawall existed then. Under the same circumstances today, someone would call the EMS, but none of us had ever heard of an emergency room.

"Cap Anderson was an old sea captain who now built small boats. He was waterproof and rustproof and coped with whatever he encountered with his own resources. He probably could have amputated my leg and put a wooden stump on it. As it was, he poured a bucket of saltwater over the wound and a bottle of iodine into it. I still have the scar."

I must have been less confident of my sailing ability than I chose to admit. I bought a copy of Calahan's *Learning to Sail* and read almost all night.

Friends came to the T-head with champagne for the launching. One bottle was broken over the bow. Another we drank as the Dutchman sailed us to our slip in the overloaded boat. We named our boat *Tontita*, meaning "Little Crazy One," referring more to ourselves than to the craft.

Marg had to go out of town for several weeks. I was in the boat every hour I wasn't working.

I didn't weigh enough to balance the boat when the wind was blowing hard, as it usually does in these waters. A postman who hung around the T-heads when he was off-duty weighed about three hundred pounds. Without mentioning that I wanted ballast, I persuaded him to sail with me.

Each time I started out into the bay in the narrow opening between the T-heads, the marina office cut off my wind. My boat would begin to slip leeward into the hull of a sixty-five-foot headboat, the *Gulf Clipper*. *Tontita* would bounce repeatedly off the hull of the heavy boat. This annoyed the captain as would a persistent mosquito. Every time he saw me putting my sails up, he began choosing salty epithets to shout at me.

I was eager for Marg to return home to enjoy the boat with me. Soon after she did, Bill Weller threw a party for the Press Club in the marina and boatel of a new canal subdivision he was developing across the bay at Ingleside Cove. Marg was too busy to sail across with me, but joined me there. We started taking friends on boat rides.

One man, who assured me he was a good sailor, took the helm. He let *Tontita* make an uncontrolled jibe, which caused the boom to slam across the cockpit. He then fell on the tiller and broke it in two.

We had to get the boat back home the next day. Jimmy Goldston, a marine engineer and good friend, owned Northshore Marina nearby. In the marina was a shop that he had leased out and to which he did not have a key. Always accommodating, Jimmy broke into the shop and fashioned a makeshift tiller for us.

As we sailed back across the bay, winds came up. Waves got high. The tiller kept coming out of the rudder post. The boat careened around in an erratic way, taking on water.

Marg had sense enough to be frightened. I gave her a tin can and kept her bailing. Somehow we made it across. When we approached Corpus Christi Marina, cruising boats were racing. I tacked so that I would not cross their course. Stopping just short of threatening to slug me with the bailing can, Marg said, "Get me to dry land—now! I mean it!"

We reached the slip. She stepped out on the dock, shaking, no color remaining in her face. The skipper of a boat in the next slip put Marg in a deck chair and gave her a glass of brandy. When she had strength enough to stand, she threw up her arms, looked over at *Tontita*, and said, "She's all yours. I never want to see that boat again. Bon Voyage!"

I got my comeuppance. Chris Wenger, a professional skipper, and I had become friends. He was accustomed to large yachts. I showed him my boat. He stepped aboard, off center, and the boat almost flipped over in the slip.

"This is an unsafe boat," he said, "too tender to stay upright."

"Not at all," I retorted. "It has never turned over."

The next time I sailed *Tontita*, Chris was watching. She capsized. A shrimper on a nearby boat pulled me onto the deck of his trawler, reached over, grabbed *Tontita's* mast, and righted her. I stepped back into my boat and sailed to the dock.

Chris didn't have to say "I told you so." I had been audacious, but now I was subdued. When small-craft warnings were flying, I could no longer ride the crest of my ignorant bliss back to safety.

By this time, I had recognized the waterfront as a place where I would work as well as play. I interviewed Jack Creveling, a local automobile dealer and civic leader who had formed a tourist bureau. He described for viewers an industry new to South Texas that would diversify the economy and give more financial stability to this area. I stayed with this story, and in the years that followed it unfolded much as he had predicted. Increasing activity on the waterfront offered endless graphic opportunities—yachting, sport fishing, commercial fishing, birding, swimming, water-skiing, and other forms of recreation.

When I was growing up, most of the boats on Corpus Christi Bay had been small, many of them homemade. Starting in the 1960s, large, handsome yachts appeared. Many were racing, not only on a triangular course within the bay, but on a circuit to Houston and to Mexican ports.

The yacht club had been a dinky structure on a barge tied up in the marina. A handsome clubhouse was built on the L-head. Meals served in the dining room were prepared by a French chef.

This was a time of prosperity. Inflation was rising, but there was too much affluence to notice. The waterfront had become a liquid asset for an area with a new mission: attracting tourists, navy retirees, and others who would come, bring money, and enjoy.

I started taking time off to sail. Something within me was suggesting that I recognize that disturbing trends were occuring in the news industry, but I was not yet ready to acknowledge that the compass course I had been on in life was not going to take me to any destination I wanted to reach. I did know that when I got out into Corpus Christi Bay and there were no other boats or people near, I enjoyed hearing the water splash against the boat and watching the dolphins play, finding that I could exist devoid of deadline pressure.

28

The Oilman and the Skipper

One of the most controversial figures to emerge from South Texas was oil tycoon Oscar Wyatt. I watched with breathless suspense as he launched himself into the risky oil business, and then he went into orbit while all the cool heads in the industry were betting against him.

Oscar devised a means of producing fields of shallow gas wells profitably, fields that prosperous oil men had written off as uneconomical. Long-established oil men kept telling me he would go broke any day. I had to ask, "Then how does it happen that, when there are crashes in the oil field, those predicting his doom have losses and Oscar always comes out richer by far?" I liked the man and rooted for him.

Chris Wenger was the skipper of Oscar's yacht. In 1963 Chris and I were married, and I became a part of Oscar's corporate family.

Oscar's sons spent a great deal of time in our home, as Chris taught them sailing and other water sports. One son, Doug, and I became close friends. He is now an attorney and, with a partner, owns an oil company headquartered in Vietnam. I receive e-mails from him from all parts of the world.

The Oilman and the Skipper 127

Chris Wenger and Oscar Wyatt (second and third from left) and crew.

Oscar moved his headquarters from Corpus Christi to Houston after losing a debate with local officials over the location of a dam. Oscar warned that the site they selected would not provide the water supply necessary for future industrial growth, which proved to be true.

I seldom see Oscar now. When I do, he is exactly the same person he always was with me, no pretense, affectionate, considerate. I miss him. There never was a slow news day when I lived in Oscar's world.

Oscar's career has never hesitated. He established Coastal

Corporation and expanded it into a diversified international industry. His reputation, known widely in Texas, spread across the United States. Stories about him began to appear in the national press. When the Shah of Iran was critically ill, Oscar's planes flew the necessary flights between the Houston medical center and Iran to attend to His Highness. When President Nixon opened up the door to China, Oscar was one of the first entrepreneurs to walk in and make deals. He brought back a 707 jet that had been in Chinese passenger service and converted it to a luxurious flying office and apartment, a junior version of Air Force One.

On familiar terms with all the potentates of the Arab countries, Oscar had easy access to Saddam Hussein when Americans were held hostage in Iraq and as the Gulf War was approaching. Oscar paid a visit to Saddam and flew his countrymen back home to safety. The U.S. State Department was highly annoyed that he was meddling in foreign affairs.

When Chris and Oscar raced sailboats, I'd fly on a Coastal plane to the destination site to join in the parties. After one race, to Tampico, Mexico, Chris and one crew member, Larry Urban, set sail back to Corpus Christi.

Oscar piloted the plane that flew me home. He put the plane on automatic pilot and was making coffee when I walked down the aisle, accidentally knocking some papers off of a chart table and stepping on them.

"You are walking on a ninety-million-dollar deal," Oscar grumped, then laughed and explained. "Sinclair Refinery is shutting down their plant in Corpus Christi. Mayor Ben McDonald asked me to buy it and keep it open so the city won't lose those jobs. I'll probably do it. It's my town. I ought to help them when I can."

Oscar never did seek credit for things like this that he did for Corpus Christi. He didn't get it, either. People were much more generous with their criticism. I came out with a good scoop on the saving of a refinery and multiple jobs.

Oscar had a thirty-six-foot sailboat hull built on the Thames in London and shipped as deck cargo to Mamaronek on Long Island Sound in New York. Chris spent several months there, supervising her fitting-out. Oscar told Chris to hire a truck and driver, put the boat, named *Serendipity*, on a truck bed, and bring

The Oilman and the Skipper 129

her from New York to race in the annual Corpus Christi-to-Houston Yacht Club Regatta.

John Connally was Texas governor at the time. He had been a friend of mine when I was in journalism school and he was in law school.

Before the sailboat started its overland trek, Oscar called the governor for a small favor—to contact the governor of every state between Texas and New York. Connally told each of those governors that the truck carrying the boat was coming through his state on a holiday weekend, overwide, overweight, overlong—all slightly illegal. Each governor was asked to assign a staff person to be on duty twenty-four hours a day to avoid delays when the boat was in his state.

Chris traveled in a rented car in front of the rig. When a trooper pulled them over, Chris took his name and number before the trooper drove off with the truck driver under arrest. Chris called the governor's office from the next telephone. Within a short time, the truck driver was back in his seat and a police escort was provided to the state line.

This was a cliffhanger of a news story. An update on every newscast reported *Serendipity*'s progress, which was also plotted on a huge map in the oil-company office. Millions of dollars may have been made or lost in the oil business that weekend. No one noticed. Everyone was moving pins around on the map, laying odds as to whether the boat would get here in time for the race.

Each time Chris called in a location, a conference call was set up to my office or house so I could join in the conversation. It was the only time in my life that I knew where Chris was at every moment.

The boat was scheduled to arrive about 5:00 Sunday afternoon. Awaiting her on the L-head were a large dragline to lift her into the water and about twenty people ready to rig her.

Hours passed. Word came that the boat had reached Victoria, but the clutch had gone out on the truck. Oscar drove to Victoria and awakened a friend who owned a truck line; he brought another flatbed to the scene. The boat was transferred to it.

When the new transporter started to roll, the headlights and taillights on the truck malfunctioned. Oscar drove ahead of the truck, substituting the headlights of his car as illumination for the caravan. A Texas state trooper stopped them. Instead of making an arrest, he gave them an escort. It was 5:00 in the morning when the trooper, Oscar, Chris, and the boat rolled onto the L-head. A tremendous shout went up from the exhausted gang of waiting yachtsmen.

In the New York shipyard, Chris had numbered and coded each item of rigging so that there could be no question about where to attach every stay, shroud, sheet, and other appendage. As day dawned, a fleet of rubber-soled shoes jumped back and forth from land to deck, and deft hands made connections.

Other racing boats were tacking behind the starting line by the time the mainmast was in place on *Serendipity*. Her motor, which had never been started, turned over immediately when Oscar touched the ignition switch. The boat left the dock while part of the crew was still stepping the mizzenmast. A penalty was automatic, because the engine was started after the signal had been given for boats to be under sail only.

Before the boat was out of hearing distance, Oscar called to me, "Get us water, food, bedding, everything we need to survive on this boat for two days."

I stood, appalled. What exactly did a racing crew need for two days and nights at sea? And how would we get it to them, since they were already underway? As I started my car, Truman Arnold, Oscar's right-hand man at Coastal, drove onto the T-head. Accustomed to dealing with crises of international proportions at any moment, Truman accepted this as a normal part of a workday.

"Don't worry," he told me. "I'll take care of it." Within a short period of time, a helicopter was on its way to sea with all essentials.

I headed for the naval air station. The public information officer had arranged for me to fly over the race on a Coast Guard plane and shoot pictures. I was put in a harness with a tail attached to a shackle on a track in the bulkhead of the plane. Crewmen opened the escape hatch. I leaned out to shoot as we made one pass after the other over tiny boats under spinnaker, their wakes sparkling in the sunlight, diminutive in the vastness of the Gulf of Mexico.

I was waiting at the finish line in Houston; *Serendipity* came in second. Oscar was mad. I said, "Oscar, second place is phenomenal under the conditions. You're a sore loser."

He looked at me with a special smile he had when he was sharing something confidential. "Good losers don't win."

The Oilman and the Skipper

The day came when Oscar did not have time to sail. I hope that in whatever he does, he finds the joy that he did in racing sailboats. I think back to a time when I flew to Houston to get a boat ready for a race. A limousine met us at the airport and took us to the Houston Yacht Club harbor. We were swabbing the decks and singing sea ditties when Oscar and Bonnie, his wife at that time, came alongside. Bonnie said, "Think about this a minute, Oscar. You have all the money. They have all the fun."

29
And Then There Was Celia

The wind gauge broke when Hurricane Celia's blast reached 180 knots. Who knows how much stronger gusts blew. The force shredded lives and devastated landscapes. Neither I nor my life would ever be quite the same.

I'd weathered many hurricanes. When I was a child, I tried but couldn't stay awake for all-night family hurricane parties. Working on newspapers in Angleton and Rockport, I followed hurricanes up and down the coast, in winds that would whip rain gear off me and shred it. It was exhilarating to buck the elements and come through with stories so strange they were hard to believe, which hurricanes always produce.

Then, in August of 1970, there was Celia.

By this time, Chris and I were living in a house we had built on a bluff at Ingleside Cove. Weather Bureau predictions were that this hurricane, a small storm of little concern, would make landfall the next day at Houston. We were having an engagement party at our Ingleside home for a colleague of mine, Fran Steele. It was a warm, clear night. Guests helped Chris carry the boat-box up from the pier to avoid damage in case of rising tides. Otherwise, we gave the storm no thought.

The next morning, I checked the weather wire, which said the storm had turned but was not a serious threat. I put together a newscast, which was driven to the transmitter by Gene Looper.

Between the time Looper left and noon, Celia, a languid storm, had aroused herself. While everyone was still in denial, she became a huge blob on our radar. Suddenly undergoing a total personality change, she turned into an angry sea monster moving at submarine speed. She was coming here!

Chris picked me up, and we drove around to see what was happening. On the waterfront, boat owners were desperately trying to haul out their crafts. Too late.

I was spinning the radio dial when KEYS put out a bulletin: "A tidal wave has inundated Aransas Pass and is moving this way."

A little more digging and I learned that a drunk, who thought it would be a good joke, had called KEYS and reported the tidal wave. KEYS sent the bulletin to wire services, which carried it across the country.

There was no tidal wave, but there was a hurricane. Gale winds were blowing by now. Carrying a movie camera, I walked up the stairs to the ground floor and began shooting pictures of the first evidence of the storm.

Our radio studio and combined radio and television news bureau was in the basement of the Showroom building. On the first floor was a furniture store. On the other side of a parking lot was the Wilson building, where our business offices were located, on the eleventh floor. These buildings overlooked downtown Corpus Christi and the bay.

Within a remarkably short time, debris was blowing past me in hurricane-strength winds. A square of plywood blew so close that it almost cut my throat. In this maelstrom, I felt dead-calm, almost indifferent. I kept shooting film.

Bricks were popping off the Wilson building and blundering their way through the air. Wilson-building maintenance men were wearing garbage cans over their heads as protective helmets. Bricks hit the cans with metallic thuds.

There was little traffic when I first began walking around. Soon there were only occasional police cars or other emergency vehicles, then nothing at all. Rains began. I ducked into the Wilson building and started walking upstairs; the elevators were no longer running.

At each floor, I would look out the windows. Parked cars were being bombarded by projectiles and crushed by falling walls. The rain was too hard to be able to see any distance. On the fifth-floor landing, a typewriter blew past me and out the window. Most other sounds were drowned out by harmonics of glass windows shattering.

I couldn't get to the eleventh floor. I went back down. Night was approaching, and it was already dark. Making a dash for it, I ran from the Wilson building to the Showroom. Display windows were blown out. I could see mattresses stacked far enough back to be dry.

Later that night, some of the staff and I went up to the Showroom and brought down mattresses on which to sleep. Mr. K said we could be considered looters. We found peacetime ethics irrelevant.

There was no light or electricity. We could not broadcast. Police broadcasts and public-service stations, along with the other commercial stations, were all off the air as well. During that night, there was only one voice on the air, that of Andy Cook, manager of a radio station in Kingsville. Andy continued to talk to anyone with a battery-powered radio who could listen. Afterward, Andy would always be known as "the Voice of Celia."

Lying on a mattress in the dark basement, I had no idea whether Chris was alive or dead. Whatever happened to the rest of the world, I expected Chris to make it. A sailing yacht skipper has to be ingenious to survive. He'd find a way.

Those of us on the mattresses ceased communicating with one another. We felt isolated, as though the whole of humanity might be wiped out. We had to rethink our whole existence. All we had taken for granted before was no longer valid.

Before daylight, the winds and rain subsided. I stood at the door at the head of the stairs with my camera. As soon as I could see shapes silhouetted, I began shooting. Normally, drizzle and gloom hang on after a storm. This morning, the sun came up in a clear sky. The wind was dead-calm.

I stepped out into a surrealistic world. No other person was in sight. Every building I saw was heavily damaged. Streets were so full of rubble, it was hard to tell where they began and building sites ended. There were no sounds to hear. I walked in a trance, feeling neither horror nor compassion; I didn't feel anything.

I had walked many blocks before a vehicle approached. A panel truck, with "Salvation Army" written on the side, was moving toward me a few yards at a time; a man walked ahead of it, clearing a path. It stopped beside me, and the driver handed me a glass of orange juice and a sandwich. I realized that I had not eaten since breakfast the previous morning.

More importantly, here were two other survivors. Not only were they alive, they were out there helping people, apparently the first entity to pull itself together and go into action.

The truck moved on. As I ate my sandwich, I began humming the tune of "Sit Down, You're Rocking the Boat," from the Damon Runyon play *Guys and Dolls*. Runyon had a way of making us laugh at ourselves.

I began to organize my thoughts, figuring out ways I could get information to the networks and news services, with the help of a ham radio operator. After those hours of ennui, I was revving up my energy, much as Celia had. I changed my tune to "Luck be a lady today!"

I headed back to the station with assurance that I knew what needed to be done and how to do it. Soon after I got back, Chris walked in. The roadway between Corpus Christi and Portland was flooded, so he had driven on farm roads from Ingleside in a circle around low-lying areas, moving fallen trees, tin roofs, and other parts of buildings out of the roadway to allow passage.

In a matter-of-fact way, he told me his story. After all the windows were shuttered in our house, he had shoved against the French doors the little upright piano, with its candle holders, that came with Father's family from England. Fragile things of value Chris fit into a walk-in closet in the middle of the house.

He kept one window open at all times on whatever side of the structure was in the lee, to release pressure and keep the building from exploding. In the dark, blindfolded house, he listened to sounds that were Wagnerian in their amplitude. A roof off a boathouse and many unidentified flying objects sheared off the tops of trees that surrounded our house; the trees took the brunt of the wind and saved our home.

When a sudden silence replaced the caterwaul, Chris realized that the calm eye of the storm was passing over. He ran out the kitchen door and down the bluff and waded out into the Cove, where he had secured our sailboat with three anchors. It had sunk and filled with sand, which was holding it on the bottom, safe from the wind. Looking around, he saw that neighboring piers had been torn apart by boats that came loose from their moorings and rammed through all obstacles.

Three blocks away, Marilyn Cochran and her husband stood under a stairway in their home on McGloin's Bluff, the highest spot on the Gulf Coast. Their entire house, except for that stairwell, had blown away.

Out on the highway, Verle Boring, his family, and employees of his convenience store entered a walk-in beer cooler for protection. When they dared to emerge, the cooler was the only part of the structure still standing.

I wanted to put my story about all this and more together, ready to air when electricity came on and transmitter repairs allowed broadcasting and telecasting. In our basement news bureau, all our typewriters were electric. There was no electricity. At home, I had a portable manual.

However, movement around the area was limited to prevent looting. When I got to Ingleside Cove, armed National Guardsmen refused to allow me to enter the subdivision. Military, in my experience, were unpredictable. At times they used common sense, and at times they were inflexible.

I had learned from being on the scenes of plane crashes and other disasters that there were ways to get around them. A marine, with rifle at the ready, had once shouted at me at a crash scene, "Stop or I'll shoot." I didn't, and he didn't. I wasn't too frightened of these guardsmen at the cove.

Two state highway patrolmen were nearby, standing on the north shore of the cove. I'd always found troopers to be cooperative. I walked over to the patrolmen and explained my need. I pointed out my house on the east shore, not too distant.

One of them told me, "If you want to swim over there, we'll cover for you. " I agreed. They moved their patrol car so that it would shield me from view. Walking toward the guardsmen, they pointed out something in the opposite direction, distracting them long enough for me to jump in the water and swim out of sight.

At the house, I put on dry clothes. Then I picked up my typewriter and walked down the road back to the highway. When the guardsmen saw me coming, they looked puzzled but made no effort to stop me. I waved good-bye to the troopers.

Looking across Corpus Christi from any height, scalped trees were a depressing sight. All of their leaves had been blown off. Trees sprouted new growth in a false spring in August.

Nancy Heard Toudouze sent me a check with instructions to plant an oak tree that would not shade us in our lifetime, but that would cast its shadow on future generations and replace one of the fallen ancient oaks.

Disasters unite and also rip apart. At the Cove, winds tore at lives with tornadic force, and pieces of some lives could not be fit back together. In the period of storm recovery, three different couples, all of whom were dear friends in the closely knit small population of the subdivision, separated and traded spouses. While the winds blew, each person's mortality must have made itself felt. What had passed for living, and relationships that had been acceptable when life was routine, were no longer valid. Everywhere was new life.

As I worked through the tremendous number of facts that I needed to compile and verify as a basis for my storm story, a totally unrelated thought introduced itself. I might be coming to the end of twenty-one-year career in electronic journalism. Such a radical suggestion shocked me. Why would I think such a thing?

I finally admitted to myself that the possibility had been stirring within me for months, but I had been unable to conceptualize it. Celia was a finale closing out a significant phase of my life.

This was not a rational decision, but an insight, a perception. In following months, I would think it through and make that choice intellectually. News, and specifically television news, was moving in directions I did not want to go.

There was no longer a good balance of positive and negative. News had become largely superficial. Little opportunity was afforded to go in-depth, to give listeners and viewers information to make difficult decisions on their own. I no longer believed that every story I wrote was the most important one I had ever covered.

As these realizations forced themselves on me, I kept working. Feeling had begun to return to me, relieving the numbness of disbelief. This was much like what people describe after a near-death experience. What is important becomes perfectly clear to you. Everything inconsequential is trashed.

30
Guarding the Turf

I left television news. An opportunity opened up to do something I had always wanted to do. I went to work for the Coastal Bend Council of Governments to help put in place lines of communications between governmental entities and provide the public with accurate information about regional issues.

As a reporter, I had become aware that lack of communication and cooperation among local government entities was creating expensive duplication of efforts and preventing accomplishment of what needed to be done. Dr. Jean Richardson, president of Del Mar College and Chair of the City Charter Commission, searched for solutions.

When John Connally became governor of Texas, he recognized the need in every part of the state for local governments to network and plan on a regional basis. The governor created planning regions across the state, with planning commissions known as Councils of Government. Participation was voluntary. As a practical matter, governments that did not join were at a disadvantage in receiving grants and other benefits. Dr. Richardson and I hoped this was the answer we wanted. John Simer, acting director of the newly organized Coastal Bend COG, asked me to come aboard as the communications coordinator.

Guarding the Turf 139

Hosting weekly television and radio programs, I also wrote a column carried by weekly papers and published newsletters and reports. I was on the road more often than a traveling salesman, sitting down with mayors, county judges, and others whose enthusiasm would be necessary if this were to work.

I knew that my greatest problem would be dealing with "turf," slang for the range of authority or influence of a person or group of people. Turf is one of the reasons it's hard to take action in government, even on something that everyone wants. Officeholders and bureaucrats too often are afraid to trust one another or to make any change that might diminish their authority or empower someone else.

As I traveled around the region, my first effort was to alleviate the fears of city and county officials that some new level of government was going to impose its will upon them. It was slow going. Gradually, they realized that the COG was not a government in itself but an extension of each elected governmental body. The elected officials of cities and counties controlled the Council and determined what mandates it would carry out for them.

Smaller governments could receive technical assistance that they could not afford at the local level. Governments of all sizes could work together in the COG to reach a consensus, then combine efforts to deal with issues that don't stop at county lines, such as crime, epidemics, pollution, and economic development. The COG could coordinate projects and government grants for programs addressing such issues as aging, criminal justice, 911 emergency communications, and economic development.

One of the quirks of my life was the fact that I spent more time on the air after I left television than when I worked for a station. While handling communications for the COG, I hosted a half-hour television program on KRIS and a fifteen-minute radio show carried by most of the stations in the region; both were entitled "State of the Region."

Every city and county in the region had representatives on the Council and on advisory committees. These men and women were leaders in their communities and took pride in discussing them on the air. Before putting on a show, I spent time in the community, learning about it and shooting a picture story of it.

Much of South Texas was ranch country, but that did not make one area like another. The county spokesmen who were my guests brought the ambiances of their home territories to the shows.

When I introduced Ben Glusing on the air, he brought to viewers much that they didn't know about Kleberg County. Glusing, banker and attorney for the King Ranch, a former state representative, and a founder of the COG, was intimate with the day-to-day workings of the famous ranch, such as its museum, in which the Caesar wildlife exhibit told an incomparable Texas story; and with research into such South Texas specialties as cactus and pink grapefruit.

On location in Refugio, I enjoyed shooting pictures of historic homes built in Victorian, Georgian, Greek Revival and Texas Dog Run architectural styles. A *dog run*, my audience learned, separates two wings of a house, allowing any breath of air to blow through each room. The streets had interesting names such as Palsuela, Ymbación, Federación, Empresario, and Purísima.

At that time, Refugio was a town with many philosophers. One of them, Lawrence Wood, was a favorite guest on my show. He was a member of the COG's Resource Conservation and Open Space Development Committee. His ranch was laid out for wildlife conservation. Sections of trees and brush were left in a natural state at regular intervals so that deer would always have protection nearby as they grazed. A corner of each field of grain was left unharvested for birds. Ponds were located on the birds' migratory path.

He spoke out on the air in advocacy of the good earth and of individual enterprise. Like most Texas ranchers, he deplored governmental interference in his life.

Another of the philosophers was Hobart Huson, then in his nineties, whose home complex included a library building with one of the state's best collections of Texiana. Hobart would talk to me on the air about the border dispute between Nueces and San Patricio counties, which is still unsettled after twenty-five years. He was the attorney for San Patricio County.

In contrast was Brooks County, where 90 percent of the residents were Hispanic and 80 percent were on welfare. County Commissioner J. M. Alaniz spoke so softly that the engineer in the television control room had to ride gain on his mike, but he spoke from his heart about his community.

My first guest from McMullen County on the radio program

was Mrs. J. C. Craine, a widow who succeeded her husband as county judge. She ran her own ranch out of the back of a pickup truck, with ranchhands only at certain times of the year. She was shy about being on the air, as she had never been in a radio station, but she offered to make me a deal. She asked, "If I come into town to do a radio show, would you take me to a mall?"

I agreed, and she enjoyed shopping. When we got to the radio station and I introduced her on mike, she froze. The expression on her face was that of a person who had witnessed a heinous crime and believed herself to be the next victim. The show was a monologue. I asked questions and answered them. At no time did she speak.

In contrast was the next McMullen County judge, Claude Franklin. In preparation for a television program, he drove me around his ranch, showing me, among other things, an abandoned uranium mine. Uranium had for a time brought prosperity there.

When we arrived at the ranch house, we learned that a stallion had gotten in with the mares. Franklin's mother, who was in her nineties, had the situation under control. She was standing in the middle of a corral, whip in hand.

Judge Franklin's greatest interest as he talked about his rural county was bringing a clinic with a nurse into the county seat, Tilden, where no medical assistance was available. In fact, until the COG worked out an arrangement with a small telephone company, the county sheriff had no telephone at his home. Ways were also found to connect his office to state law enforcement by teletype, and the county to an emergency radio network. This was the first action in the COG's development of a sophisticated 911 system in the entire region.

Judge Franklin was a history buff. Audience response was good to programs on early days in McMullen County, when the hills had been known as the badlands, where stagecoach and train robbers hid out.

Those killed in a shootout in front of the Old Stone Store, now a museum, were buried in nearby Boot Hill. All those buried there died of either violence, the plague, or childbirth; none died of old age.

Claude Franklin died, and his wife, Elaine, was named county judge. She was one of the most beautiful, intelligent and perceptive, women ever to represent her county on the COG. The Franklins fought for the environment, preventing issuance of permits to allow industrial waste to be buried near the river that ran through their ranch land.

Radio and television-program guests were invited from other counties and from the state to talk about what was going on in local government outside our region. One of these guests was Ann Richards, who would later be governor but at that time was recognized as a progressive Travis County commissioner.

The night of the program, she was in Corpus Christi attending a County Judges and Commissioners Association meeting. I picked her up in the bar of her hotel, where she was the center of attention of a group of good old boys having a lot of laughs.

This was a short time before Ann announced publicly that she had a problem with alcohol. I realized while driving her to the television station that she had been drinking more than a little.

In the studio, with bright lights on us, it was even more obvious that she was not enunciating clearly and was laughing at inappropriate times. I worked hard to avoid anything that would hurt her politically. I thought twice about every question, trying to anticipate her answers. That was the longest half-hour that I ever spent in front of a camera. Finally, the cameraman started counting me down, and I gave thanks that nothing untoward had happened.

Those programs were a way of letting people compare notes with their neighbors. They were part of our efforts at the COG to create awareness of how much could be accomplished if we worked together on regional issues, while appreciating our diversity. I was no longer a legitimate member of the news media, but in the position I held, I think I did accomplish a few of the things that I had seen as crucial while I was a reporter. I still write a weekly column for the COG and handle some communications.

Certainly, turf problems still exist, and the COG is limited in how much it can help local governments serve their electorates economically and effectively. A number of remarkably capable men and women from the counties of the region have served as chair in the short lifetime of the COG. They have made a difference.

31
Integrity and Power

My relationship to the men and women in the power structure of the Coastal Bend was quite different as a COG staff member working with them than it had been as a reporter. Two of the most engrossing and influential men that I worked with were Hayden Head and Judge Bob Barnes.

As a reporter, I heard a lot about Hayden Head, all of which made me skeptical of him. He was the attorney who represented most of the heavy industry in South Texas. He, it was said, was the political power behind the throne in the Coastal Bend, and along with H. E. Butt and Sid Richardson, had more clout with the state government than any other South Texan.

The first time I remember talking to Hayden Head informally was at a cocktail party in some high-rise. We were looking out over city lights and the bay, discussing the rising crime rate.

"We could stop crime, you know." He paused. "All we have to do is shoot anyone caught breaking the law. You get a parking ticket—bang—you're dead. "

He looked at me with an expression I was to get to know well. A wide smile told me he was sharing a joke with me. His eyes disputed that. Serious, his eyes stared directly into mine, deciding how I was reacting to what he said.

At the Coastal Bend Council of Governments, when I was coordinating intergovernmental information, Hayden served one year as chairman and at all times was on the executive board and the Environmental Quality Committee, so I was in constant contact with him. Although people and words are my profession, in some ways I found Hayden's personality impossible to describe or even understand fully myself. He was extraordinarily brilliant and he was ever gracious to me. I grew to feel real affection for him.

Obviously, he was an important man with great demands on his time, but he was accessible and never appeared to rush. This was a quality I found not infrequently in men who actually had power, as contrasted to those who wanted the public to think they had.

He could draw forth the clarity of words in the English language with as much sensitivity as a musician's touch on harp strings. If I wrote something that I particularly wanted to be fine-tuned, I'd take the article to Hayden's law office. He would speed-read, marking this out and writing that in as he went along. Each time, it was incredible to me how easily he injected the precise meaning into sentences so there could be no misunderstanding of the intent of the text.

He was that good at everything he did—and witty. In a hot debate, he was as pleasant to and considerate of those strongly opposing him on an issue as he was those providing him support.

Hayden seldom missed a meeting of the Environmental Quality Committee. Committee membership was balanced, with industrialists and environmentalists represented about equally. Hayden contended that industry could operate economically without detriment to the environment if those from both sides were reasonable and reached consensus. It appeared to me that he played a big part in achieving that balance. There are always things that are not obvious, especially when dealings involve state agencies.

In negotiations, Hayden had a way of making you feel he especially liked you and appreciated your strengths, which he found to be many. At the same time, there was some unfathomable quality about him that set him apart, even at the times you were feeling closest to him.

Most would-be officeholders knocked on the door of Hayden's law office and presented their credentials. It would be an exaggeration to say that it was hard to be elected if Hayden opposed you. It would be accurate to say his support would be of great help.

Solomon Ortíz, who had been county commissioner and sheriff, was one of the first Hispanics to receive a nod from Hayden. He went to Congress. This proved to be a wise choice. Solomon has served his district consistently and with good results.

Hayden was a pilot and was flying his own plane when it crashed and he was killed. A terminal in the Corpus Christi International Airport, where no international flights landed, was named after Hayden. He probably would have chuckled about that. He used words so precisely and here an "international" airport was named after him when it did not have any international flights.

I missed Hayden. I felt sad that I had lost someone I liked and admired. No one knows what differences his death made in the politics, the economy, the future of Texas.

Hayden and Bob Barnes, the Nueces County judge, worked closely together. The judge discussed with Hayden any important decision to be made. He was not, as I saw it, subservient to Hayden. He had respect for Hayden's opinion and valued it.

Barnes was one of the best and certainly the most unfathomable county judge I ever knew. He was outspoken, never moderating his words to appease another person with a different point of view. As an officeholder who would not lean a fraction of an inch to gain a vote, he was an endangered species.

In his way a loner, he told me that he had no friends. Actually, he had many friends and admirers, who wished they had his courage. He was humorous, knowledgeable, and intensely interested in everything going on in the world.

Barnes' father was accountant for the Port of Corpus Christi when I was growing up, and his father and mine were friends. I first remember Bob Barnes as a bond salesman attending meetings of the commissioners' court, then as a member of the court, and finally as a judge.

Mathematically, he was a whiz. Give Barnes a budget and he could spot a speck of dirty politics in the darkest corner of a journal page. Corruption in its most everyday forms infuriated him.

He discovered illegal practices in a mental health agency that received some county money. The language in which he described the agency director's lack of vigilance with tax dollars was as blue as a cloudless Texas sky.

Barnes could change quickly from one mood to another. He might express vicious judgment of a wrongdoer, then swivel around in his office chair and pull a book of Emily Dickinson's poetry from the shelf. The voice that had been that of an angry judge was now that of a gentle dreamer. He would read aloud of the splendors of nature or the promise of immortality.

He and his wife, Mary, loved music, from opera to Linda Ronstadt. They traveled hundreds of long Texas miles to hear a concert, then drove back home through early morning hours to save the expense of a hotel room. Whether spending his own money or traveling on an expense account, Barnes did not waste.

He served as chairman of the Council of Governments. Attending COG conferences in Houston or San Antonio, he would fly up with a garment bag over his shoulder, hang the bag in a closet in my hotel room, pick it up in time to change for dinner, and after dinner fly home. It didn't matter to him who saw him coming in and going out of my hotel room or what they assumed. He knew what he was doing, saving money by changing there and not paying for a room for himself.

Actually, Barnes loathed government. He reduced it to its simplest form whenever he could. He would have done away with most of it, probably even his own job if that had been possible. Yet he kept running for political office as a way to change the system.

Barnes and I differed on this. I, too, wanted to change the system, but I wanted to do it by informing the public and encouraging voters to make changes. Never did I want to be personally involved in politics.

I was approached once by a political party spokesman and asked to run for a county office.

"No," I told him, "I agree with Harry Truman. If you can't take the heat, stay out of the kitchen."

His response was, "My wife doesn't like to cook, either."

Barnes loved that story and sometimes used it to illustrate what he thought of politicians. About that time, Barnes decided to run for Congress. There was no way he could win. How could anybody expect to go to Congress when he says nothing but the truth,

Integrity and Power 147

compromises nothing, and makes no effort to tell voters what they want to hear?

He was one of the few politicians who really liked reporters and cooperated completely. He grumped when I got out of the news business to work for a lowly government agency. He didn't hold it against me, though, as he was always loyal to the many friends he said he didn't have.

His campaign manager asked me to make a speech at a rally for him. I asked John Buckner, executive director of the COG, whether it would be out-of-line for me to do this. He said, "It's your neck. If you want to stick it out, be ready to defend yourself on any charge that may be made that you have violated a COG policy of being politically neutral."

I thought for a while and decided that it would be worth losing my job to send an honest man to Congress. I made the speech. No one could complain that I influenced the election unduly, since Barnes lost by a large margin.

While Barnes was chairman of the COG and on the executive board, I reported to him frequently on work being done. Incongruously, Barnes loved gossip. At one time, the COG imported an executive director who had an entirely different management style than those who preceded him. He moved us from small, cramped offices to an entire floor of a high-rise with windows overlooking a roof garden. Instead of one secretary, there were now four or five sexy young women who looked like models, doing their nails or making personal phone calls. One brought an Afghan Hound to work each day to lie like a throw rug in front of her desk.

Barnes could hardly wait for me to arrive at the courthouse to describe developments. I did not have to exaggerate to keep him enthralled.

Ruth Gill was a Corpus Christi city councilman. (She and I agreed that through time *man* had been used as the plural in English for men and women, and neither of us would use the awkward *councilperson*.) An attractive woman, she had as much integrity as Barnes. She was elected the first woman chairman of the COG. Even before she took office, she had dismantled the place as effectively as a tornado, but with much more finesse. When the debris was cleared, that executive director inclined to live high on public funds was gone, and Buckner was promoted into the job.

Buckner, an environmental engineer, was a realist, not a dreamer, as are some planners. As an administrator, he saw to it that the staff carried out the policies of the elected representatives on the COG to the nth degree. He did his own typing. No secretary. He watched every cent of COG money as carefully as he did his own and was a match for Barnes in his economies.

Following the procedure established while the previous director was there, I reported to Barnes everything the COG staff was doing under Buckner's direction. Finally, Barnes interrupted me. "Buckner's way of doing business is so dull. Isn't there anything more provocative going on in that office that you can tell me about?"

Even though Buckner would go to great lengths to respond to the request of a representative to the COG, he made no effort to change his lifestyle, even at the risk of boring Judge Barnes.

32
Ancestral Grounds

Travel has always been important to me. The first trip I took across the Atlantic was as a guest of France when Air France inaugurated a flight from Houston to Paris by flying a planeload of journalists to the French capital. That was an event.

I decided it was time to cross the Atlantic again. I reduced my work schedule at the COG, which allowed me the luxury of traveling. This time my destination was England, land of my father's people.

Germaine Thallman, daughter of a Swiss senator, and I had become close friends when she was married to an American naval officer who was stationed in Corpus Christi.

Then living in Basel, Switzerland, Germaine suggested that we meet in England, where she had a cousin, Bill Winter, who was a master at Eton. We could make his flat our headquarters for day trips, and we could take the boat-train to the Continent for more extensive travels.

My plane landed at Gatwick Airport, and I took a train into Victoria Station. There, Germaine met me, and with her was Bill Winter. England personified? Bill Winter was big and lusty enough to embody the entire empire. Steeped in tradition and pageantry, he seemed to feel no doubt in his mind about anything. To know him was to fathom the being of a people who dominated much of the history of the western world.

He stood at the entrance of the Grosvenor Hotel in Victoria Station, almost filling the doorway from top to bottom and from side to side. All I knew about Bill before I flew to England was that he was a master at Eton, that he sent word I was to bring floor-length gowns, as we would be dressing for dinner, and that he was addressed as William Winter, Esq. My dictionary defined *esquire* as a male belonging to the gentry and ranking directly below a knight.

Bill, Germaine, my luggage, and I crowded into his little Porsche. We sped through traffic in a lane that Bill somehow cleared for us, much as God rolled back the Red Sea for the Israelites. We passed every landmark I'd ever seen in pictures of London. My quest had begun. I wanted to know more of the origins of my own country as inherited from England and develop some understanding of this unique country with an island mentality and a worldwide reach.

Conversations would give me the greatest insights into British characteristics. Fortunately, in academia, in England and in the States, there are still dialogue, ideas, and conversation.

The first discussion I heard was of the pros and cons of the monarchy versus a republic. We were lunching at Bill's flat with friends of his, Sir Michael and Lady Helen Oppenheimer. The only Windsor indiscretions mentioned were the divorce of Margaret and Charles' abdication. Much was trivia. "Princess Margaret is unpleasant. She has bad manners. She's rude to servants who have been in the household for years."

Conversation that night showed me a much more scholarly side of the interests of Englishmen who were educated in public schools and widely traveled. We ate dinner in the Eton dining room. Many of the guests were art historians invited by Bill in recognition of Sir Michael's interest in early Italian Renaissance art. I was intrigued by a small man who was physically deformed. He told a story that ended with the question, "Do you know that dogs always bark at cripples... anything different?"

The next morning, Bill took me with him to a class he was conducting on Eton silver. Here, boys in their early teens talked about each valuable piece that Bill removed from a vault: a teapot, urn, plate, or flatware. They compared patterns and silversmiths and the changing accouterments of the aristocracy during a sequence of eras.

Anscestral Grounds 151

The boys developed lifelong ties to Bill. When grown, the Eton graduates would scatter throughout the empire. Bill would take sabbaticals and visit the "old boys" as his own.

We talked a great deal about education in various countries, its shortcomings and advantages. The most compelling comparison to me was the structure of university systems. At Bill's old college, Trinity, at Oxford, I read the schedule of lectures posted for the day. Students had no required classes, instead choosing lectures they wished to attend and searching out what they needed to know in the library, with assistance always available.

Did this require more maturity than our controlled schedules, or develop more initiative? We explored the ins and outs of this conversationally as we walked along the bank of the Thames.

Religion, as it is wont to do, raised the most ire of any subject. Bill told me how uncomfortable he is attending an Episcopal church in the United States, saying, "Contents of the new prayer book are near blasphemy. Passing the peace is almost obscene. I protect myself in your churches, sitting behind a post where it is difficult for strange women to run up and hug me."

We attended a service in Eton Chapel, Bill dressed as he always was on campus, in a morning coat with tails, dark pants, and his scholar's robe. As we entered, he pointed out, "The Italian frescos on the walls were unknown until the paneling was removed. Remember, Eton was a school before printing was invented."

During the service, Eton boys read intercessions that they had written themselves. They asked God to intercede in the problems of the Jews and the Arabs, and in the affairs of Princess Margaret.

Most of the time, Bill was in the best of spirits as he interpreted England to me, opting whenever possible to recognize the traditional and acknowledge no change. We watched Prince Charles play polo on the Windsor field and heard a grand estate on the decline go on the block at Sotheby's Auction House.

Germaine was with us part of the time, and at other times took care of affairs of her own. When Bill was otherwise occupied, Germaine and I shopped in London and saw much of the city.

She was with us at Saint George Chapel in Windsor Castle when we listened to chamber music, surrounded by Knights of the Garter, ribbons across their chests, escorting their ladies in ball gowns.

After a performance of *Othello* at Covent Gardens, the three of us dined at midnight at an elegant little café in Mayfair. Bill conferred with the wine steward about what we should drink with each gourmet course.

Driving home from one of our evenings out, Bill began teasing me about the lack of culture in "the Colonies," as he always referred to the United States. I asked him about something that I found confusing.

"Bill, why is it that tradespeople and trainmen always say to Germaine with great respect, 'How may I serve you, madam?' but always seem to find me amusing and say, 'What can I do for you, Love?'"

Bill's only answer was, "Oh, but you are most amusing, my dear."

One day, while I was staying at Bill's flat in Eton, he decided to let me solo. He agreed to let me strike out without a chaperon.

I wanted to find traces of my great-grandfather and his family, who lived in Bexley Heath. I boarded a train at Waterloo Station in London, failing to ask whether I had to change trains at any point to reach my destination. When the train got to the end of the line, I still had not seen the Bexley Heath Station.

Getting off the train, I approached a railroad man who was walking along, swinging his lantern, and told him my predicament. He said, "Get back on the train, Love. I'll be with you in a minute."

Finishing his rounds, he came in and sat down beside me. I told him where I wanted to go and why. He explained to me what train to catch back toward London and at what station to change.

He gave me directions in a way that only an Englishman would, with great feeling for history and genealogy.

"You don't want to go directly to Bexley Heath. It would be difficult to find anything if you did that. Get off at Bexley, the county seat. Walk to the foot of Gravel Hill. There you will find Hall House, a grand place. It was owned by Woolsey before it was confiscated by Henry VIII.

"It is now a hall of records. City directories and voting records for every community in the county for every year of modern history are to be found there. Note down the addresses of your family members. Then walk to the corner and catch a double-decker bus marked 'Bexley Heath.' Get off at the clock tower. With the information from the records you can locate family homes."

Arriving at the foot of Gravel Hill, I stood and thought of

Thomas Woolsey, the Roman Catholic cardinal who was charged with treason when he failed to obtain for Henry a rapid divorce from Katherine of Aragon. It was then that King Henry established the Anglican church. Revolutionary Americans, wanting no part of anything English, changed the name to the Episcopal Church. Thus it was that my Anglican grandfather read Bible stories to his Episcopal granddaughter during my early childhood in Austin.

In Bexley, a walk through the extensive garden of Hall House, with its sculpted shrubs, took me into the building, where a local history librarian directed me to the correct area of the stacks. Reference books were neatly arranged by thousands of years.

Quickly, I found the references I needed. I walked to the corner, where the double-decker bus stopped exactly as the trainman said it would. I rode the short distance to the clock tower in Bexley Heath and got off. Following leads from the information I found at Hall House, I was able to walk directly to the location of the "Joseph Jordan Knight home, Mera Lodge, on May Place Road, four doors from Providence Place, between Milfield and Public Hall. "

Mera Lodge, as such, no longer existed. This area was now a close. Standing on what had been my great-grandfather's property, I recalled pictures I had seen of Joseph and Martha Knight and envisioned how they might have looked getting out of a carriage here.

Taking impressions of those scenes with me, I walked down Broadway to Christ Church, where my grandfather was a lay reader. In back of the church was the cemetery. It was huge. It had not occurred to me that in a small town with a thousand years of history, the cemetery would be as big as that in a large city at home.

A funeral was ending in the cemetery. The vicar, Angus McFarlane, big, hale, pink-cheeked, with vestments flying, breezed across the churchyard. I stopped him to inquire how I could find the graves of my ancestors. He directed me to the park department in city hall, back down Broadway.

In city hall, a clerk served me a cup of tea as I searched files on microfiche. Then I returned to the Old Plot in the cemetery, Grave Number 2097. To save space, bodies were buried one above the other. There, one at each level, were buried Great-Grandfather Joseph Knight, age 90, 1899; Martha Knight, 95, 1913; Ellen Knight, 93, 1937; and Harriet Knight, 87, 1949.

Harriet was my great-aunt; I had exchanged letters with her

when I was a child. She had sent me a tortoiseshell-and-brass tea caddy and a picture of her home, a cottage almost hidden behind a yard bursting out all over with flowers. I knew the address, 24 Pickford Road. A woman at the bus stop told me to catch Bus 122.

What I didn't know was that there was a Pickford Lane, Pickford Road, and Pickford Close, and I got off at the close. The house number I was looking for was not there. A little dandy of a man came striding down the street, wearing plaid pants with a look of knickers, a herringbone jacket, and a golf cap.

I said formally, "I beg your pardon. Could you assist me?"

His eyes twinkled at me from under his cap. "How can I help you, Love?"

I told him the address I was looking for. He laughed cheerfully. In heavy cockney, he said, "But you got off the bus at the 'close.' You are looking for the 'road.' Come along. I'll show you. I'm going that way anyhow, to buy my fish and chips. Friday, you know."

We all but skipped down the sidewalk, talking as confidentially as two old friends. I thought I recognized a house, and he pointed to that one as he stopped. "Here you are, Number 24. You take care of yourself, now, a young lady from another land, all alone." He tipped the cap and was on his way.

Standing in the garden, I listened to the silence. I felt that a form of communication was in place between my father's family and me that had not been there before. I now had mental pictures of these home places that I could always recall, and I could people them as I chose in my mind.

When I was back in the colony I had always referred to as "Texas," I knew I was where I belonged. I'd continue to live and write in the Texas tradition, but I knew I'd go back. England had a lifelong hold on me.

After that trip, I saw news in a different context, as a part of what was happening outside our country, in the world. English newspapers, television, and individuals discuss issues important in all countries. World news receives much more attention in England than in this country, and particularly in Texas, where we are learning only slowly how to be global.

33
Forgive Us Our Differences

It was a louse that inspired Bobby Burns to say, "Oh wad some power the giftie gie us to see oursels as others see us." Two hundred years have passed since he wrote that, but there is still the question of whether we have moved any closer to seeing ourselves or others without distortion.

Among the most important stories that can be written about South Texas are multifaceted depictions of the Mexican people and people of Mexican descent. Vast numbers of Texans have formed opinions of Mexican people based solely on those they see in this country. Immigrants living in barrios or harvesting crops are, to them, the only Mexicans. These are for the most part poor, illiterate people who came to the United States because they were told of the quality of life here but have no idea how to access it.

Reporting for both television and newspapers, I have written in-depth stories that show a little of what Mexico really is. The first story I covered about Mexico examined the surprising growth of heavy industry in Monterrey, which previously had been only a romantic tourist town. I went to Monterrey and found endless material for a story I wrote on that city's maturation.

On such trips into Mexico, I was interviewing industrial executives and government officials in high positions. The concept that many South Texans have of Mexico does not include people such as these: educated, intelligent, and successful.

Granted, Mexico has not competed business-wise with countries such as the United States. Their government has penalized them with corruption that is devastating. Even so, a middle class has grown and exists.

Mexicans measure success according to different values. They enjoy an affectionate nature, music, dance, a relaxed attitude. Many would not trade the slower pace of their lives for greater financial gain.

The Mexican consulate in Corpus Christi was at one time a favorite hangout for reporters. The diplomats were highly educated men with a great deal of experience. Men of this caliber and their families were not a part of the social life of the Anglo population, and such men did not come to the minds of many people when they heard the term "Mexican."

There certainly was not a language barrier. The diplomats spoke English impeccably. Luis Avalero, one of the most charming of them, told me, "English is fantastic in its precision. I always want to do business in English. I make love only in Spanish."

When I am around Mexicans such as these, I become more convinced that we should be teaching children from every ethnic background in several languages from the time they are in kindergarten. If we could all talk to one another without effort, and read each other's newspapers and literature, that would have to make a difference.

Victor, one of the diplomats, had high expectations for his life. He planned to return to Mexico to run for governor in a state where his father had once held that office.

I asked him how he felt about the *mordido,* or "the bite," whether he would take kickbacks from contractors who bid on roads or other capital-improvement projects. He thought a moment, then said, "Probably—it's the custom. But I would always make sure the company which received the contract was the one that would do the best job and give the people their money's worth." This was to Victor a critical shade of difference.

Forgive Us Our Differences 157

Such contrasts must be dealt with if we are going to move nearer to accepting one another and our differences. In Mexico many buildings leak and are never quite finished. The designs are so original and the colors so lavish that the Mexicans enjoy them, put buckets under the leaks, and forget it. What is lacking in quality control is found in more than full measure in talent and creativity.

Ingenuity is everywhere. Engineers of Guanajuato rerouted a river that ran under their town and frequently flooded it. The dry riverbed they converted into underground streets and parking areas. Cars rush along underground while pedestrians stroll unimpeded on cobblestone streets above.

The most obvious course for Mexico to begin to raise people out of poverty would be population control, but religious beliefs eliminate that as a possibility. Talk to college professors, members of old families of wealth, or people moving into the upper middle class with the industrial expansion. Everyone recognizes the need for social change, but no one has foolproof solutions.

I had heard discussions about Mexico in my own home since I was a small child. When we lived in Austin (until I was nine), my father was sales manager for Tipps Engine Works, traveling a territory consisting of fourteen states, Mexico and Central America. He would deliver a large engine to be installed in a cotton gin in a hacienda, then remain as a guest of the family to supervise the installation of it. He spoke good Spanish and delighted in life on the haciendas. He would tell me how generous the Mexican people are. "Never," he told me, "admire a painting or anything of value in a Mexican home. The next time you are in your own home, you will find it awaiting you there, special delivery."

In the U.S., we are always in a hurry. In Mexico, even trains don't run on time. On one trip, as our train stopped in desert nothingness, I watched a conductor jump off the observation car and race down the track in the direction from which we had come. I asked why. The answer was that a train was coming up behind us, and the conductor was rushing to stop it before it hit us. Couldn't we move forward? No, there was a train ahead of us broken down on the tracks. No one was particularly disturbed. There is a certain fatalism in Mexico.

Whenever I traveled on a Mexican train, I always went forward into the second-class car. There, among goats and chickens, children played. They threw arms around me if I joined games. All showed love, none inhibitions.

Riding a train through Copper Canyon, we were off-loaded onto a bus that was to take us to a mountain lodge. A fuel pump went out. The bus caught on fire. Flames were extinguished. We went on up the hill on the bus with a boy holding a bottle containing gasoline being siphoned directly into the carburetor. All of us might have been burned to death. We weren't. It was an adventure. Isn't that what travel is supposed to be?

A medical doctor I was interviewing in Saltillo explained to me that he never bought a new car, as it would quickly disappear, either entirely or one part at a time. He bought a new motor and put it in the battered body of an old car, which no one bothered to steal.

When I cross the border into Mexico, I become one of them. "*Que sera sera.*" We leaders of the world in the United States insist that all other countries reform and be like us. In the rush of meeting deadlines on this side of the border, I promise myself, "Someday I'm going to be more like the Mexican people and simply enjoy."

34

The Onion King

Small vintage newspapers targeted for a literate readership have found their niche in print history. Fortunately, I was involved in such a publication, late in my career and late in the time such rarities could survive, because the mass media in the 1980s were gradually excluding all but the commonplace.

A friend, Sam Keach, told me that he and two other weekly newspaper publishers planned to establish an upbeat weekly on the affluent southside of Corpus Christi and asked me to join the team as managing editor.

The timing was right for me. I could continue to write my weekly column, sent to smaller town newspapers of the region by the Coastal Bend Council of Governments.

The new weekly, *Southside Today*, was intended to give subscribers all sides of issues of substance and the stories behind the stories. We would not emphasize or sensationalize any single facet of community life, but learn and pass on reliable information about whatever local developments would be relevant to our readers.

Let's face it, we were idealists. Feature stories and good photography would have a place along with hard news. The humorous and whimsical side of living in our midst would find its way onto the page, but we would respect privacy on subjects personal in nature.

Reception of the little paper was one of spontaneous combustion. Readers let us know that this was the news they wanted. They read it avidly and talked about it. Advertisers heard what they said and came to us. In staff meetings, there was elation. We were zooming into the future, our little tabloid assuming size and status.

We were, that is, until the publishers of the daily paper noticed that the insignificant upstart had become more than an annoyance. The daily, part of a profitable chain, could afford to drop advertising prices as low and as long as necessary.

Each of our advertisers was offered a vastly larger circulation at a minuscule price. No sensible businessperson could refuse. As rapidly as we had grown and our advertising increased, it skidded down the balance sheet to an unacceptable bottom line.

Southside Today found itself in the position of a sailing vessel when it is "tide rode." In Lydia Ann Channel near Port Aransas, when the tide is ebb, strong currents override prevailing winds. A boat, instead of lying downwind and tacking, rolls in a trough.

The paper lasted for two short years. However, I enjoyed the experience immensely, and it was while working on this paper that I became acquainted with one of the most remarkable people I have ever had the opportunity to meet.

If it had not been for *Southside Today* and Cecil Burney, I would have missed out on one of the most moving experiences of my life—getting to know Abe Katz. During our university days, Burney had tipped me to stories to send home from Austin in the column I wrote for the *Caller-Times*. Later considered the state's most knowledgeable attorney on banking laws, he was still a stringer for me. Cecil called and suggested I write the story of Abe Katz, "the Onion King."

We met for our first interview in his office downtown in the Katz building. He spoke easily, with neither pretense nor false modesty. A short man, he had large, strong shoulders, big hands and feet. He was wearing a crisply ironed white dress shirt and dark slacks. At first, the conversation skipped around as he told me unrelated stories.

The FBI investigated him when he was reported to be buying arms and ammunition while the state of Israel was organized. President Harry Truman ordered the case closed soon after he recognized Israel as a nation.

Abe Katz.

I confirmed this with George Denton, the FBI agent in charge in the investigation, who told me, "I kept trying to learn the name of Katz's underground contact. He would look right at me with a guileless expression on his face and tell me that he didn't know the name. He was always polite and pleasant. He'd say, 'By helping chase the English out of Israel, I'm doing the same thing that George Washington did in the United States.' When the president advised me to close the case, he said Katz had made no money out of the transactions, and there was no evidence he had done anything wrong."

I asked Katz whether it had angered him to be investigated by the FBI. He said, "Anger? Anger is a waste of energy. God didn't intend you to be angry."

Katz was one of the early contributors to efforts to get endangered Jews out of Europe during World War II. He paid for a full-page ad in *The New York Times* to kick off a successful fund drive.

His accomplishments were described by Benjamin Netanyahu, Israel's ambassador to Washington at the time, in a dedication speech at a Hebrew school in San Antonio. The program listed Abe Katz and the ambassador's brother, Colonel Jonathan Netanyahu as "Heroes." The colonel was the one man killed when Israel flew into Entebbe to rescue hostages held by terrorists.

Katz's father, mother, two sisters, and niece were killed by their young Lithuanian neighbors, who had joined the Nazi party. Katz learned that terrible information from Lazar Goldberg, a childhood friend of his in Lithuania, who had escaped from the work camp by throwing himself into a river that ran through the camp. The water carried him, nearly drowned, outside the fence.

Goldberg was able to reach a farmhouse. The farmer, at his own risk, dug a hole in the ground below his barn and buried Goldberg alive in a dark, damp grave. The farmer took him food and water when possible. There he lay for five or six months. When the country was liberated, Goldberg arose from his grave. He was blind for almost a week, until his eyes adjusted to the light. For days, he bathed constantly with buckets of water to rid his body of an infestation of lice.

When Katz told me the story, he cried, then smiled at me. "My parents taught me it would be an unforgivable weakness to allow despair to obliterate joys of the life God gave me."

We went back to his earliest days, when Russians were occupying the small town on the Lithuanian border, where he was born. His older brother, Max, received a law degree in Russia. By the time Katz was of school age, Germans had occupied the country and did not allow Jewish children to attend school. Abe was taught the Torah by his father, a Rabbi and Biblical scholar. Abe taught himself history and philosophy.

On the Sabbath, the family always had an especially good meal. Abe's mother packaged portions of food, and Abe delivered meals to families in need. His father told him, "You are obliged to make a living, but beyond that you must accumulate deeds, not wealth."

During World War I, when Abe was nine, German soldiers confiscated the family home, giving them forty-eight hours to get out. What they could carry, they put in the wagon. On the road, they were in a line of wagons and refugees on foot, headed north. The only food they had were potatoes they dug from fields they passed. Compassionate property owners looked the other way.

Americans landed in Europe. Katz said, "Angels from heaven! They filled acres of land with their bodies. They won the war. They didn't occupy any countries. When they went home, they didn't take anything from anybody." Katz was the greatest patriot in his adopted country of the United States that I have ever known.

He continued. "Twenty years later, there was Hitler. The sons of the Americans who freed us in 1918 arrived. When the war was won, they spent billions of dollars to put Europe back together economically. Such a people! There are no other kinds like them. Their generosity! If it were not for the United States, the world would be a jungle. American-born people can't appreciate it."

Until he was twenty, Katz lived with his family. "Lithuania was a small country, overpopulated. Jewish families were usually large. When Jewish sons reached a certain age, they were like birds who hatched and got wings. They took off. God had blessed the world with a country called the United States of America."

Abe and his thirty-year-old brother, Leon, went to Mexico to live until they could get visas to enter the United States. Abe first spoke Lithuanian and Hebrew. Then he learned Spanish. This was the third of seven languages in which he would become fluent.

He and his brother worked as street peddlers in Mexico. In

1928 they were able to cross the border legally into Laredo, and Katz went to work for a dollar a day selling shoes.

He met a man from New York named Mankof who came to South Texas each year to buy onions. Katz made him a deal. He would work for room and board.

It was the right place and right time. Onions had been grown primarily in California and the Texas Winter Garden. South Texas would become the biggest onion-growing area in the United States for the next twenty years. One hundred thousand acres of dry cropland was planted in onions. The first crop of onions in the nation was harvested here each year.

For one season, Mankof and Katz lived in the historic Nueces Hotel on the waterfront in Corpus Christi. The season was beyond all expectations for both of them. "Before Mankof returned to the East Coast, he gave me a hundred-dollar bill, riches in a land of opportunity. He arranged with two local produce men to give me a job."

Most of the truck farmers in the Coastal Bend were growing cabbage. Katz's new job was to call on farmers in the region and convince them that there was money in onions; to sell them onion seed; and when the harvest was in, buy the onions to be shipped across the United States.

With his first weekly paycheck of $13, Katz opened a bank account. His statement arrived with a one-dollar service charge. The young immigrant walked into the office of the president of the bank and introduced himself. "I can't afford to pay that charge right now. However, I am going to be a wealthy man, and I'll make it worthwhile to this bank if you will forgive me the charge for the present."

The banker made a judgment call and agreed. Twenty years later, Katz and two other investors built Corpus Christi's first shopping center, then sold it for a substantial profit. Katz took his share of the money and deposited it, interest-free, in the bank for a period of time; in doing so, he repaid the debt manyfold.

Prospects were good until rains came and kept coming. Lands flooded, the onion crop was lost, and the company that Katz was working for went broke.

A New York produce company offered Katz a job as their manager in Robstown. He went to work for them and persuaded the railroad company to give him a packing shed on the tracks. He

The Onion King 165

concentrated on onions but also dealt in spinach, beets, carrots, and cabbage.

Katz was twenty-eight years old when he made a trip to Dallas to meet with an associate in the produce business. He met the man's eighteen-year-old niece, Doris.

"She was the most beautiful woman in the world, and she still is. I stood only five feet, eight inches tall, and she wasn't impressed with me. We were married ten weeks later. I rushed the wedding up so I could combine the honeymoon with a business trip to New York."

"How did you convince her to marry you?"

"I sold her a bill of goods. She buys it to this day."

As he and his wife made their home and reared their children, Katz spent days in the field, selecting and buying onions, and nights in the sheds until 2:00 or 3:00 in the morning, readying vegetables for shipment.

At the same time, he was studying the history and government of his adopted country in quest of citizenship. He went before a magistrate to be examined. A railroad executive and a broker were his witnesses. They agreed that it was a good thing they had been born in this country; they could never have passed that exam. In those years, citizenship was a hard-won prize.

When the produce business again went on the skids, a Robstown banker urged Katz to go into business for himself. Katz had saved six thousand dollars, which he put up as leverage, and the bank set up a line of credit. The banker told him, "You are the only man in the produce business who isn't broke. This bank will extend you unlimited credit."

Katz commented, "I'm sure that banker is in Heaven. I have been praying for him."

World War II ended. The government encouraged farmers to switch crops from produce to grain, which could be sold around the world to feed hungry people. Milo became the crop of the Coastal Bend. Onions were still grown in the Rio Grande Valley. Katz moved his business there.

In partnership with Roy Shapiro, Katz established Valley Onion, Inc. The company farmed 6,000 acres of onions, shipped across the United States and to Europe and Canada under the brand name "Blue Baby."

Katz commuted between his business and home on a ten-passenger King Air Jet that the company owned. His wife, Doris, suggested the plane was an extravagance. Katz agreed and rode a Continental bus to the Valley for the work week and back home on weekends.

Katz had always grown the Bermuda onion, from Spanish seed produced in Bermuda. These onions rotted if a big rain fell before harvest. Onions harvested would hold up only a short time in storage. On a trip to Israel, Katz learned that a grower named Ben Shemen had developed a strong onion, the Menshemen, that did not rot nor deteriorate rapidly. It was, however, so hot that it would burn your tongue.

Katz brought home five kilos of the Menshemen and planted a demonstration plot on his farm. Rains came, the onions were harvested and dried out one hundred percent sound. He shipped some to a customer in Michigan, who told him two months later that the onions had not rotted.

Katz took his data to Dr. Leonard Pike, a plant breeder at Texas A&M University. With six other South Texas onion growers, including the controversial McAllen mayor Othal Brand, Katz made a commitment to pay for cross-breeding research on what they called "the Jewish onion." For twelve years, they financed breeding, quality-control, and promotion.

The result was the Texas Grano 1015Y Supersweet. The number 1015 is the planting date, October 15, in latitudes west of 22 to 36 degrees. Y stands for yellow bulb. Dr. Pike calls these the best fresh-market, short-day onions in the world.

The Texas Produce Growers Hall of Fame was established in the Rio Grande Valley. Katz was the first person inducted. He was given the title "the Onion King." Texas onion growers had, in one year, made $77.8 million, establishing the onion as the top moneymaker among vegetables in the state.

Not long after that, Katz was investigated by the federal government for a second time. This investigation was by the Internal Revenue Service, which advised him that "No one contributed to 'that many' causes." They found they were wrong about that. His philanthropies were extraordinary. His secretary showed me a huge cardboard box in which they kept all letters of solicitations and copies of responses in case the IRS came back again.

When Katz was eighty-two, his family persuaded him to cut back on his labors. He sold Valley Onion to Florida interests of Duda, a Czechoslovakian-based produce giant with worldwide operations.

He was actively involved in politics. He supported, with time and money, whatever candidates he believed to have integrity and the interest of his country at heart. "Sometimes I supported Democrats, sometimes Republicans. What difference does it make? They are all Americans, aren't they?" He never failed to add, "God bless America."

35
Transitions

How many lives we live. When *Southside Today* closed its doors, I decided I would work primarily on the North Shore of the bay instead of commuting daily to Corpus Christi. I continued my part-time work with the Council of Governments and began to write features for the *Aransas Pass Progress* and *Ingleside Index*. Dick Richards, who had been an owner of *Southside Today*, owned these two weekly papers. He wanted profiles written called "People of the Bay Area," and I enjoyed doing that. I have written for his papers ever since.

This opened up for me an entirely new way to explore the waterfront. These two North Bay communities were originally fishing villages, with Ingleside a produce center, as well, and Aransas Pass a retail center. At the same time I made my transition, the fishing industry was making a most difficult change.

Conservationists were exerting pressure to regulate commercial fishing, in the belief that waters were being overfished. Sport fishermen were on their side. Commercial fishermen had been hard-hit by Celia, which destroyed many of their boats, and by rapid climbs in fuel prices. Except when they had years with exceptionally good catches, they were not making a living.

This is the kind of story on which I think reporters should be concentrating. What is true and what is myth about natural resources, at present and in the future? What is political and what is necessary for conservation when new government regulations come into being?

I spent a great deal of time with fleet owners, with fishermen, and with spokesmen for conservation groups. One of the most dramatic meetings I ever attended was held at a VFW Hall in Rockport.

Muscular men, accustomed to dragged in fishing nets, filled the large meeting room. An elderly, frail man spoke to them in the language of those comfortable in air-conditioned boardrooms and communicating on the Internet, a language the fishermen found disparaging.

To me, the confrontation they enacted took on universal dimensions. The man at the podium was William Negley, a San Antonio millionaire. The audience was composed of American and Vietnamese shrimpers whose industry was being destroyed, their livelihoods disappearing.

The shrimpers, like many in other industries who depended on hard, physical work to support themselves, were finding that their labor was no longer enough.

What was happening in the room was a global trend, but as a Texas phenomenon it had deep resonance. Around the world there are two images of Texans. One is of the cowboys, oil-field roughnecks, fishermen: tough, independent men who stand tall in the great outdoors. The other is of men whose power is not in physique but money, accumulating vast wealth in oil fields, chemical plants, and other businesses and industries. Both were realities in that room. The shrimpers were being told that they were an endangered species, no longer a part of the Texas myth.

Negley, the speaker, was closely associated with Perry Bass, longtime chairman of the Texas Parks and Wildlife Department, whose son now holds that position. Negley and Bass are both sport fishermen, the commercial fishermen's adversaries.

Negley was proposing that the Texas legislature pass a bill taxing sport fishermen and using the revenue to buy out commercial fishermen, paying each twenty-five thousand dollars to get out of the business.

A bearded shrimper stood up. "My boat cost almost two hundred thousand dollars. How do you think I am going to make a living?"

Negley replied, "We are exhausting natural resources. Remember what happened to the buffalo hunters when buffalo became extinct."

Wiley Morgan, owner of two fish houses, uninterested in buffalo, stood up. "You are messing with a lot of people's lives. We don't understand why. This is our heritage. One boat and one license represent many people. When you start taking things away from people, they get upset. You are going to put people out of work and on welfare, and the Parks and Wildlife Board is right in there with you. These people are not going to lie down."

Negley stood silent, a tall man who looked as though he were shrinking with age and using breath that was almost exhausted to preach his beliefs. For the moment, he did not defend himself.

Morgan continued, "Bankers are refusing to lend fishermen money that they need for cash flow. The bankers believe you and the parks board will put the fishermen out of work, so they wouldn't be able to pay back any debts."

Negley spoke then, describing how fishermen in cold, northern waters had been bought out to prevent overfishing. (Rich Tillman, an environmentalist and a marine agent for Texas A&M University, told me that in warm waters there is a new crop of shrimp every year; thus, the situation is different.)

Negley spoke of polluting water and damaging the environment. A skipper rose and said, "We are environmentalists. Our livelihood depends on the environment. Who are you, a millionaire, to tell us what to do? This is America!"

Voices around him chorused, "Don't get personal. Keep it down." The meeting didn't end. It stopped.

I went up to Negley and asked him, "Why are you doing this?"

He looked at me sadly, but with pride. "As a private citizen, I'm trying to help these people. My family has always been interested in the public welfare. My great-great-grandfather was a secretary of the nation of Texas when Sam Houston was president. My mother was the first female in the Texas legislature. From what I hear and read, I think these people are at risk. I'm offering a solution."

Such inability to find a common denominator is polarizing people here, as various differences between people are doing in every part of the United States. Negley is a symbol of a special interest offering himself as a civil servant for the good of the people, sure that he knows best. The people he is trying to help see him as exercising clout that big money uses to reshape government and the economy to their own advantage.

Negley had a theory of how government could solve a problem. The fishermen believed that Negley and the government *were* the problem.

36
Women at the Helm

Recreational sailors were among the many "People of the Bay Area" I've written about in my feature series for the *Ingleside Index* and the *Aransas Pass Progress*. A subject to be handled carefully in these stories was that of the macho skipper.

Male-female relations take on a diffferent dynamic at sea. I've noted on many occasions that the mildest-mannered man can become a bellowing tyrant when he strides the deck of the sailing ship he commands. First mates, otherwise known as wives, make themselves as inconspicuous as possible when a sailboat leaves the dock. Next, the skipper orders everyone to move rapidly into action to accomplish all necessary tasks of getting under way. After those tense moments of departure, captain and crew-woman relax and enjoy peaceful hours until preparations start for the ordeal of landing.

Cruises with Chris were among the best times of my life. We had searched the East and Gulf coasts for the boat exactly right for us and found at Annapolis a twenty-two-and-a half-foot Sea Sprite that we bought and named *Olé*. We tied it up to the pier in front of our house at Ingleside Cove.

On many cruises, we rendezvoused with a loosely knit association of sailors brought together by Jack and Virginia Shell. Each

Women at the Helm 173

boat sailed its own course, rafted up for happy hour, then dropped back on anchor to allow scope to swing on if winds changed during the night as we slept.

My favorite cruise was to Shamrock Cove in the spring, when shorebirds were nesting. Jack led us in dinghies through small channels, far enough from shore to avoid disturbing the birds, but close enough for us to scrutinize their family life with binoculars.

As much as I loved *Olé*, I wanted a boat that I could sail singlehanded. Chris showed me a picture in a boating magazine of a "West Wight Potter," designed and built on the Isle of Wight to "potter" around in. I had once visited the yard where they are built. Chris said, "This is a boat light enough for you to handle, yet stable. If we ever find one, I'll buy it for you."

He probably thought he was safe. Neither one of us had ever seen one in the United States. It was not many weeks before I was attracted to a boat beached at Rockport Seafair. Approaching it, I discovered it was a West Wight Potter. Full speed, I ran to find Chris.

He lived up to his word. Soon, it was mine, and I was communing with the dolphins as I sailed among ships and fishing vessels down the channel from Ingleside to Port Aransas. I called my boat *Wee Lass*.

At times, two friends joined me, Claudia Jackson, assistant to the president and director of community relations for Del Mar College, and Jo Ann Luckie, director of special populations at the college. We developed our own feminine ways of doing things that the men accomplished with brute strength.

Battling with wind on nearly every cruise, one or the other of us, while bringing a flapping sail under control, left on its whiteness a smear of lipstick. The mark was never cleaned off and remained as our signature. We talked about writing a book called *Lipstick on the Sails*.

We compiled a glossary of our own nautical terms. None of us knew anything about such boating accessories as "shackles." Claudia had earrings that worked on the same principle as shackles, and we understood earrings. Whoever needed a shackle to make a connection would say, "Hand me an earring."

Never underestimate the ingenuity of women sailors. One day, the wind changed when we were picnicking on an island down a channel too narrow to tack out. We had no motor on *Wee Lass*. Claudia and Jo Ann clamped their hands on the transom of the boat as though they were outboard motors and flutter-kicked us into open waters, where we could raise sail.

Our voyages were always leisurely and noncompetitive. Only once was I a member of a crew in an all-woman sailboat race. In the Betty Boop Race out of Bahia Marina, Carol Regnier skippered her boat, the *Noname*, while Vera Mangold handled the sails and I navigated. We were first around one mark. *Noname* had a good handicap, and even though we weren't first across the finish line, we walked away with the trophy.

I would be remiss not to mention the good sportsmanship of Carol's husband, Keith. He had competed in *Noname* in many a race and never taken first place. Despite that, he celebrated our victory so enthusiastically that it gave us all hope for recognition in the male psyche of women's sailing abilities.

37
The Scotties

I have a deep belief that no one can work up to his or her potential as a reporter, contending with the suffering and malfeasance in the world, without a dog at home. Inevitably, cynicism falls away when the dog greets you, reassuring you that the world is in good orbit and you are the pivotal center of the universe.

Ingenious minds fool around in cyberspace and international relations while I'm still puzzling about communication with my dog. I'm told that dogs don't think. Mine express themselves.

My father and I both related to dogs all our lives. Toward the end of World War II, when I learned that my father had terminal cancer and returned home, I checked the kennels and discovered a Scottish Terrier puppy available for twenty-five dollars. My father, when I reported this to him, was horrified. We had always taken in strays. "Pay twenty-five dollars for a dog! Never!"

Not long before the kennel closed for the day, Father said, "You know, if we don't pick up that dog before five o'clock, someone else might get him."

When Father died, my mother, ill with fatigue and grief, sold our house and disposed of many things, including the dog. She said she had given him to a friend in the country. Neither she nor I was

Scottish Terrier MacDuff with Launcelot Knight.

in a position to take care of a dog at the time, but I had become a confirmed Scottie lover.

Seven years later, when I first went to work for a radio station and bought a house of my own, I bought a Scottie and called him "Loch Lomond." A friend named Spunky had two dogs in a fenced backyard. Much as children are taken to a daycare center, my dog was dropped over the fence each morning when I went to work. I picked up Loch there at whatever hour of the night I got home. When he was still quite young, the dog became ill with encephalitis. He died in my arms while I was trying to drive him to the vet.

It was seventeen years later when I again decided I could no longer survive without a Scottie. By this time, I was married, and Chris and I were living at Ingleside Cove. Chris had not grown up with dogs and had no desire for one.

He was out of town on business when I read a classified ad in a newspaper. A Scottie needed a home because his navy family was moving away. As compulsively as any gambler ever headed for a casino, I drove to the address given in the advertisement and picked up the dog. The owners agreed I could take him on probation and return him if Chris was adamantly opposed to adopting him.

He was not a show dog. His head was too big and his tail was too long. But I thought him the most beautiful animal I had ever seen. He sat erect beside me in the car as we drove home. Only once did he whimper.

I named him Starboard because, like a sailboat on a starboard tack, my dog always has the right-of-way. Chris agreed the dog could stay, but added a codicil. "He'll have to stay outside. I don't want a dog in the house." Within a few minutes, he and the dog were roughhousing on the floor.

The next day, Chris built a fence and a doghouse and cut a dog door through the wall. As far as I know, Starboard never spent any time outside of air conditioning except by his own choice and never set foot in the doghouse.

Starboard was not only our house dog, but our boat dog and traveling dog. We were doing a lot of water and land cruising, and he was always aboard. He balanced precariously on the transom of the boat, surveying the expanse of water. On each trip, Chris instructed me, "If he falls in, put on a life preserver before you go in after him."

Chris Wenger and Starboard I.

The Scotties 179

Starboard was well boat-broken, so we had to anchor out near islands periodically. If he needed to go ashore in the middle of the night, I rowed him to land in the dinghy. When the wind was blowing hard, Chris tied a long rope to the dinghy and pulled us back aboard.

Starboard loved boats, but not water. He stayed in the cockpit watching for dophins. When they appeared and blew, the dog would run from one side of the boat to the other, making noises that sounded like those of a small child trying to talk. I can't prove it, but I know the two species communicated.

Starboard was extremely independent. He accepted us as his family, but he was not subservient. Guests could pet him for a short time, if they wished, but he invited no further contact. He didn't pick fights with other dogs, but if one made the slightest suggestion of a growl, Starboard was happily into the fray.

At the time, Chris was driving to Riviera Beach each day, to a yard where a boat was being built for Oscar Wyatt. Starboard went with Chris and roamed freely around the docks. Final touches were being made on the boat after it was launched and in a slip. Starboard was nearby when he heard a boat motor start. He had no intention of being left behind. Turning quickly, he ran full speed to the dock and jumped into the cockpit of the boat pulling away from its moorings.

The only problem was, this was not his boat. It was the boat leaving the slip next to his. The dog looked at the skipper and saw a stranger. The skipper gawked. A missile had landed, obviously misfired. He turned his boat around and offloaded the flying stowaway. Starboard had given new meaning to the admonition "Look before you leap."

When he was eight, Starboard became ill. The vet said he was probably poisoned by eating too-long-dead fish on our beach. The little dog became disoriented. He would walk into a wall and be unable to turn around to walk away from it. Transfusions would restore him for a day or so, but we finally had to admit to ourselves that he must be put to sleep.

Starboard II was sired by the same stud as our first Scottie. The new pup was perfectly proportioned. The kennelmaster wanted to show him, and we agreed.

The pup's hair had to grow long for a show, cut with his skirt sweeping the floor. Constant brushing and bathing were required. Starboard won blue ribbons in two shows but let us know that he disapproved of all the grooming and life on the road in a cage. We said, "No more."

The three of us did a lot of camping out on the Guadalupe and Frio rivers, canoeing and floating rapids in inner tubes. Starboard II had his own truck tube with a plywood bottom lashed into the doughnut hole.

This Starboard never did require any training. He sensed what we wanted of him and did it without protest. We didn't worry about an open gate. Starboard II had no desire to go anywhere but where we were.

The one thing he would not put up with was music. Perhaps it hurt his ears, or maybe he liked to howl along. He drowned out the sound of music whenever he heard it. Playing a tape or a radio in the car was no longer an option.

At Christmas, my church choir came a'caroling. We welcomed them into the house, forgetting that our dog had no holiday spirit. To the choir's dismay, he howled from the first note to the last.

At about the same age that Starboard I had become ill, this dog did, also. He was found to have cancer. In illness as in good health, he gave us no trouble at all. Quietly, when the time came, he went out in the yard, crawled under the bed of the camper, and died.

Chris said, "No more dogs. I can't go through this again."

I gathered up Starboard's toys, collars, food, and related articles and put them in the trunk of the car.

Chris asked, "What are you doing?"

"I'm taking these things to Jay Nelson. She has several dogs and can use them."

"Wait a few days," Chris requested. I unpacked the trunk, and within the week, we were back at the kennel to talk to Bill Justice. Bill and his wife judged dog shows all over the world. Recently, they had brought a new Scottie bitch home from England and sent her to a kennel in the Midwest to be bred.

When the puppies were born, we selected the runt to be Starboard III. His mother was an articulate dog, making sounds that you could interpret. This Starboard would also become a great communicator.

We brought him home when he was seven weeks old and still

fit into the palm of my hand. He was a beautiful dog, the smartest of the Scotties, the most obstinate, and also an escape artist.

When Starboard III was still a small pup, he leaned over the edge of our pier in Ingleside Cove, watching a fish in the water. He fell in with a splash, turned, and swam to land before I could reach him.

At all times eager to play, he would grab your hand to get your attention. When you responded, he bit down and tore flesh. He also insisted on turning over wastebaskets and scattering trash as ceremoniously as a flower girl with a basket of rose petals coming down a church aisle in a wedding.

This dog had to be trained. I found a listing in the yellow pages for "Well-Mannered Dogs." Patricia, the arbiter of canine social mores, came to our house to give Starboard, and us, four lessons.

On her first visit, she put a choke collar on Starboard, then made over him effusively. Joy! He took her hand in his mouth and bit down. She leaned into his face and gave the meanest growl I ever heard. Amazed, Starboard backed up to me and barked at Patricia.

"Quiet!" she commanded, and gave his choke collar a yank. He made not another sound and never bit any hand again.

She then brought in a wastebasket and enticed him to put his head into it. She growled maliciously in his face. He avoided wastebaskets in the immediate future.

Patricia taught him to obey commands, always on the leash. He still obeys commands when he is on a leash and knows you have the upper hand. When an unexpected opportunity for freedom opens up, however, he goes for it, looking back at you with a catch-me-if-you-can expression.

Starboard III is a dog who truly loves. All people are his friends. Pleased to have company, he is never ready for them to leave. When they do, he barks and snaps at their feet going downstairs to try to keep them from walking out the door. He also considers all dogs and cats his friends. When another dog growls or barks at him, he just wags his tail and tries to play.

He is a demanding dog. If I am a few minutes late feeding him, he barks at me indignantly. When I sit down in front of the computer, he quickly informs me of my dereliction if I fail to give him a milkbone bribe to leave me alone and allow me to concentrate.

One night, he came to the side of our bed and barked. I said, "Starboard, be quiet, we are sleeping, and we don't want to play."

He kept whining. Suddenly, we heard a loud voice shouting, "Evacuate this house! This house is on fire! How many people are in this house?"

Chris, Starboard, and I all ran down and into the driveway. Volunteer firemen and a truck arrived almost immediately. They quickly brought the fire under control.

A short in the downstairs air conditioner had started the fire. At about the same time, a shrimp boat was coming into Palm Harbor channel and docking at the marina across from our house. The mate happened to be an off-duty Corpus Christi fireman who was crewing for his father, the boat owner.

The fireman came up on the deck of the boat, sniffed, and said, "I smell an electrical fire." Then he saw smoke and told his father, "Go call 911." Jumping in his truck, he drove around canals to our house, evacuated us, and was there to help the volunteers when they arrived. Because of his experience and quick action, the fire did minimal damage.

Starboard never forgot. When we go to bed at night, he runs from room to room barking. Apparently, he is trying to remind us that it is dangerous to sleep in this house, especially since we are not insightful enough to get up and get out when he awakens us with barks as shrill as any smoke alarm.

Batteries go dead in smoke alarms. Computers crash and leave us inconsolable. Starboard III is indefatigable, always ready to protect us from mean herons that land on the rail of the deck or the paperboy who trespasses before dawn.

Starboard makes us laugh. When we are dismayed by all the terrible happenings reported in the news that day, the little dog rubs against my ankle and insists on being taken for a walk. Striding along with him, the sea breeze cooling us off, we look around us at what appears to be the best of all possible worlds.

38
The Gift of Sight

Chris and I moved to Rockport in the fall of 1992 and found ourselves living in a colony of 150 artists. Still writing my column for the *Ingleside Index* and the *Aransas Pass Progress*, I took every opportunity to talk to Rockport-area artists. Fortunately, these creative people were usually more than willing to share their perspectives. Many of them were completely immersed in the area's environment of birds, water, boats, and windswept trees.

I was especially eager to hear what Simon Michael, who established the original art colony in Rockport, would tell me. He had been one of the starving artists among the bohemians on the Left Bank of the Seine in Paris before war brought him home to the United States and a Texas military base.

After the war, the beauty of Rockport brought him here to paint and to teach. His school attracted other artists. Fishermen in this waterfront village found themselves modeling for classes of students who framed their deeply lined faces in the fluid green netting that hung from the rigging of their boats.

Michael told me, as he did his students, "Never imitate. Use your own creativity. There is no right or wrong way to see things." What he was saying had an application to objectivity in writing as well as honesty in art.

"Do not see a 'thing,' " he went on. "See through it to its meaning. Nothing is ugly. There is every conceivable color and texture in a garbage dump. You can possess anything you see because it becomes a part of you. Don't copy. Interpret what you see and feel."

Nanci Barnes introduced me to new and interesting ideas. "There are more variations in color existing in nature than we are able to see." She explained to me, "I may point out the violet and mauves in clouds in a picture to a person who until then could not see them, because that person thought of clouds only as black and white."

Nanci told me a story about natives on an island in the Pacific during World War II who came in contact with an industrial civilization for the first time. The natives could not see the boats and planes that arrived to capture their island, because they had no words for boats and planes in their vocabulary. How can you see what you don't know exists?

Nanci's husband, Al, is an internationally known artist who sails, fishes, and paints the seas of the world. He shared with me how he deals with the enormity of living and painting what he lives.

"When I see a new environment for the first time, I am overwhelmed by it. I don't sort out the information to arrive at a single image. Back in the studio, I start to remember, putting together the pictures. The information may be stored away for a long time, until it dovetails with what I am experiencing. I become aware of what I could not have known when I first saw it."

He was putting on canvas what I try to put on paper, the merging of ideas, images, and experiences.

Artist Herb Booth came to Rockport at about the same time as Al Barnes, when it was first developing its art identity. Booth told me, "Light is what art is all about. Not objects, but how they are lighted. Without shades of light, the objects would be boring."

Not only was I learning what to look for in art, but I was also grasping shared elements of communication.

Booth explained to me, "Art gives a different way to see the world and enjoy it. If children share this experience, they see how other people interpret the world, then in their own art they find their own way of looking at it."

Evelyn Atkinson is an architect as well as an artist. The detail of the draftsman is there in her work. At the same time, she is a magician creating an illuson by painting into what she sees what she feels.

The Gift of Sight 185

Bonnie Prouty is one of the Rockport artists whose works can be seen on exhibit across the nation. Her pictures portray her own spirituality, connecting people to their environment and to creation.

Another painter, Theresa Justice, regularly holds her paintings up to the mirror when she finishes them to look at the reflections. She told me that this gives her distance as the mirror enables her to see the wholeness of things, which she could not discern close up.

Abstract artist Lynn Lee claimed that in his landscapes he paints not the outside of a mountain, but the inside, the strength of it. He is a lapidary as well as a painter. He pointed out that the highlights of gem colors are created only by their imperfections, saying, "This teaches me that I don't have to be beautiful." He elaborated, "It's a spiritual experience; bringing out the beauty of the opal that the Creator put there for me makes me a co-creator."

Landscape painter Steve Russell described to me how he paints landscapes. He told me, "As I begin to paint, I throw the scene out of focus. I start with an abstract, go to the impressionistic, then into some realism. Sometimes I wish I did not have to finish a painting. A part of the energy of the abstract is lost in the evolutionary process.

"In the beginning I look for lights and darks. I don't see a blade of grass. I see shadow of color and light. Suddenly, I find out that green thing I have been painting is a tree. I start coloring in the details." He seems to jump into the deep end of life from the high board.

Jesús Bautista Moroles, a sculptor of renown, told me, "Polished surfaces do not have the life that does torn granite. Shining facets are lost. The simplest, most minimal things are best. I pass by a block of granite, in a pile in the yard, looking at it day after day until it speaks to me. Then I start chipping away, breathing my own spirit into the stone."

Creating art and writing are both ways of communicating something newsworthy about the art of living.

39
Coming Full Circle

It's been fun, being where the news is. Writing a book has allowed me to relive of the best of times. I had forgotten what a blast it all was.

When I first began the process of writing and remembering, I found myself back in Angleton in no time at all, in a back shop full of near-junk equipment. In my mind, I was curled up on a stack of newsprint, taking what today would be called a "power nap" while the Linotype was being repaired so that we could finish a round-the-clock job of getting the weekly paper out.

When I went to work sixty years ago, Texas was as much an attitude as a geographical entity. People who set the course for government and business believed in saying what you meant and meaning what you said, and in taking responsibility for yourself and for your neighbor down the road.

Reporters took seriously our role as the Fourth Estate, keeping those in control accountable, but we did not take ourselves too seriously. There was camaraderie in the courthouse and city hall. One reporter taught Marg Brown's new mynah bird (whose cage hung in her office) to say, "To Hell with the city manager." Reporters were always adversarial, but we were not predatory, as many are today. Being objective mattered to us. Some of us drank too much, living excessively both on and off the job. We dug for

Coming Full Circle 187

hard news, answers to the question "why?" as well as the other "W's." We were not news personalities reflecting our own viewpoints.

In my career as a reporter, I first utilized the medium of newspaper, then radio, and then television elbowed its way into the picture.

Newspaper stints from the 1940s to the 1990s included jobs with eight different papers as printing technology moved me from the back shop and the Linotype to stories written on computer and computer-operated presses.

Radio sent me out as a one-woman news bureau. Working with the radio stations KEYS and KSIX, I could not take pictures and had only unedited monolgue to describe events. Speaking into a microphone, I'll never forget having to contain my terrified feelings as I walked through the narrow passages in the house of a recluse that I was interviewing. There I encountered newspapers, magazines, and other articles stacked from floor to ceiling while the shining eyes of rats followed me as I moved through the semi-darkness.

Television came along, and I was able to explore a new medium in its formative stages. Etched in stone is my coverage of a speech the mayor of Houston made at a large meeting in Corpus Christi. When I moved up close to the podium, aimed my Speed Graphic at him, and touched the trigger, the bulb exploded not too many inches from his face, leaving him shaken and temporarily blinded and me with much of the skin burned off my hand. Back at the KZTV news bureau, I wrote the story of his speech, stopping every few minutes to run up to Parr's Pharmacy, where Buford Getty would cover what skin was left with ointment. Fortunately, reporters today don't have to worry about exploding bulbs on their cameras! Not too many months later, I was shooting a picture in a cave in the Champagne region of France when I turned around and saw the mayor of Houston seated at a table. "Don't shoot a picture of me," he pleaded.

When I first began attending national meetings of the News Directors' Association, it caused great confusion. No other woman was news director of a radio-television operation at that time. My registration apparently was made with initials, J. K. Wenger. When I appeared in the shape of woman, it caused some consternation. Later, when I got to know my colleagues, they told me how they had scurried around, eliminating entertainment such as x-rated films from the program.

I spent every January of my life from the early 1950s to the 1980s writing scripts and and rehearsing scenes for Press Club Gridiron shows. We made fun generously of prominent locals. Mayor Farrell Smith, an extremely serious-minded man, got up in a city council meeting one day and pontificated on what wonderful relations the city had with the navy. He was basing this on the fact that one of the higher-ranking naval officers was attending council meetings every week. He had no idea that the officer was portraying him in the Gridiron Show and was at the meeting to memorize his mannerisms and characteristics of speech.

Obviously, most of our time was not spent cavorting around a stage, but concentrating on the various subjects we were covering. While the process of disseminating news was always changing, the happenings in the territory we were covering were changing at an equally fast rate. There were constant breakthroughs in every field—government, industry, schools, medicine, agriculture—and we as reporters had to be prepared to change our attitudes.

The Rev. John Francis Wyatt, a remarkable Episcopal priest who is my friend, claims in his book *Experiencing God* that "we are all works in progress." In that I find encouragement.

Dr. Delbert Edwardson, my physician, told me recently that when you enter the practice of medicine today, it is a completely different field from what it was ten years ago. We talked about a breaking news story describing how a neurosurgeon removed half of a girl's diseased brain, then re-trained the other side of her brain to allow her to carry on a normal life. My immediate thought was that the technology is fantastic, but the phenomenal thing is the people. Psychology has discovered new continents of information. Yet, in relationships with one another, as people, as corporations, as nations, all of us are lagging behind.

Not too long ago, I was completing radiation treatment after surgical removal of a breast cancer. A cowboy from Orange Grove was taking treatment at the same time. He had a tumor that prevented his brain from sending the correct messages to his legs to instruct them how to walk. He was in a wheelchair, and during the weeks we sat and talked, awaiting radiation, he told me every day, "Sweetheart, we're going to walk out of here together." When we got ready to leave, with the help of his sister-in-law he arose from his chair, took her arm and mine, and he did walk out beside me on his own, brain-directed legs.

When we said good-bye, he added, "I'm going to miss you. We had fun, didn't we?"

I agreed.

I wrote a story for the Aransas Pass and Ingleside papers on what a positive experience it had been for me to survive cancer and learn all about miracles from patients and radiation therapists who took them for granted every day. Getting to spend sixty years in the news business is miracle enough for me.

The Bee-Picayune

VOLUME 57—NO. 21   BEEVILLE, TEXAS, THURSDAY, SEPTEMBER 24, 1942   TWELVE PAGES

BEEVILLE, TEXAS, THURSDAY, SEPTEMBER 24, 1942

Local Scrap Campaign In Foreground Here U Climaxing Junk Rally

Tonight's Program Will Be A Milestone For Beeville As Well As For Local Civilian Defense

The band will strike up the opening chords, "Oh, Say Can You See." All eyes will be on Old Glory as the Pledge of Allegiance is said. For Americans, that means something.

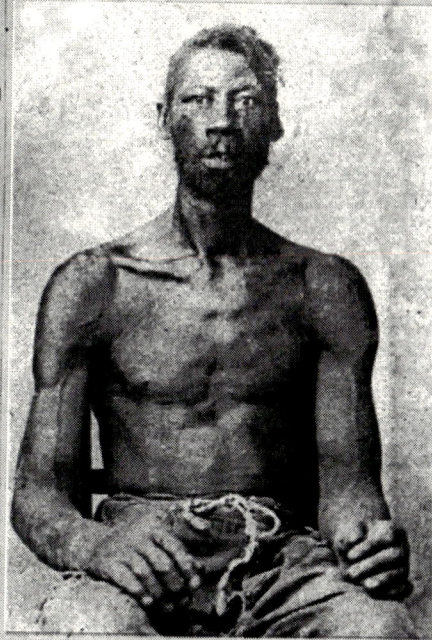

Tonight (Thursday) at 8 p. m. in Beasley auditorium, all Air Raid Wardens, Auxiliary Police, Auxiliary Firemen, and members of the Civilian Defense Drivers Corps will receive their certificates of qualification at a program with a wide scope of interest and entertainments.

"These men and women have spent several months studying and working to enable themselves to protect the citizens of Beeville in an emergency," Mayor Douglas Hermes, municipal coordinator said. "They will continue to study and to practice all late methods of home defense. Every resident of the town should show his appreciation for the work they have done and will do by attending the program and signifying that he is behind them."

"The ideas and instructions that will be brought out tonight," Mayor Hermes continued, "should be common knowledge to every citizen so that he may cooperate with civilian defense workers during an emergency and be an asset rather than a debit at all times."

Musical numbers will be furnished by the trio and the High school band, and speakers will be Robert Marshall and J. B. McAtee. The Texas Defense Guard will take part in the program.

In the audience will be many people, people determined to make sure the author of the words "Long may it wave," had more than a vain hope in his heart.

SHOWS SCARS—The above picture of Alfred Irwin, taken September 15 when he was brought to Beeville by officers, shows scars on his face, chest, and arms which he says are the result of beatings given him with an eight-foot bull whip by A. L. Shrobarcek and his daughter, Susie Shrobarcek. The Negro, unshaven, his hair long and in braids, is wearing the clothes in which officers found him and which he says are the only ones he possessed.

Shrobarcek Released on $3000 Bond, His Daughter on $250 After Examining Trial Friday

Following an examining trial Friday morning, A. L. Shrobarcek was bound over to the grand jury and released on $3000 bond and his daughter, Susie Shrobarcek, who had waived examining trial, was released on $250 bond.

During the trial, Highway Patrolman Frank Probst and Deputy Sheriff Bob Hale, arresting officers, took the stand and told the condition in which they found the Negro, Alfred Irwin, September 15, on Shrobarcek's stock farm and what the Negro had told them about the four years he worked on the farm.

The attorney for the defense, T. M. Cox, did not introduce any witnesses but told the court that wide prejudice had been aroused over what he called a possible "Quasi-misdemeanor" case. He said that his client could produce witnesses to prove that the Negro had not been held a slave. He added that not more than $1000 bond should be set as the Negro was still alive and from what he could understand "had an excellent appetite."

Maynard Porter, acting county attorney, conducted the examination of the two officers. Mr. Probst, first to take the stand, had signed the complaint against Miss Shrobarcek and her father for maiming and disfiguring which carries a two to five-year penitentiary sentence or a $2,000 fine.

The case, although tried by Judge I. N. Boothe, justice of peace, was held in the district court room because of the large crowd of spectators. Mr. Probst said that he and Mr. Hale went to the farm to investigate a report made to them. When they got within 100 yards of the field in which the Negro and Miss Shrobarcek were working, he said he could see the wounds on Irwin's back.

"The Negro was getting on a dump rake and both his back and his mouth were bleeding," Mr.

—See SHROBARCEK, Page Six

The Angleton Times
THE COUNTY PAPER
ANGLETON, BRAZORIA COUNTY, TEXAS, THURSDAY, JANUARY 29, 1942

JUDY AND OPIE—Juliet Knight gathers an item from Tom Prather, president of the Beeville Junior Chamber of Commerce, as she makes her rounds on "Opie" the bicycle she has named for the O.P.A.

Two Drown As Car Plunges Into Oyster Creek
JTK

Barcus Brown And Clara Javes Victims Of Crash Wednesday

ANGLETON—After knocking twelve four by four rails from the Oyster Creek bridge and high diving into the water, the car in which Barcus B. Brown, formerly of Alvin, and Clara Javes of Angleton were riding, sank in mud five feet under water where both occupants were drowned. The accident occurred on the Freeport-Angleton highway, Wednesday at 3:45 a. m.

W. A. McGee, deputy sheriff of Freeport, said he was not able to remove the bodies from the automobile until nearly six o'clock at which time the car was pulled onto the bank.

A fisherman who lives on the shore of the creek, James Wall, was getting up when he saw the lights flash and heard what he said sounded as if it were an explosion. The horn was blowing when the car went off of the bridge, and Wall said he could still hear it making a "blubbering" noise under the water.

The fisherman jumped into the creek, but was unable to get any door open in the automobile. Only the back wheels were above the water with the car lying on its top.

The automobile was badly mutilated with a four by four jammed through the radiator and the front seat, although neither of the bodies was cut. They were taken to the Freeport Funeral Home.

Brown, a guard at the Dow Chemical Company in Freeport, had worked until midnight. Three weeks ago, he moved to Angleton from Alvin.

Funeral services will be held Friday at 2:30 p. m. in the Alvin Methodist church with the Rev. A. E. Burns officiating and Rev. S. F. Wright and Rev. Geo. W. Springfield assisting. Pallbearers will be the Dow Police and the Alvin Fire Department will be honorary pallbearers.

Brown is survived by his widow, Mrs. Opal Brown; one son, John, both of Angleton; his mother, Mrs. Mary Dendy, Alvin; two half-brothers, Luther Dendy, Alvin and Robert Brown of Galveston; his father, Pierce Brown, Galveston; one brother, Samuel P. Brown, Galveston and one sister, Mrs. Fred Woodward of Austin.

A County-Wide Newspaper Serving the Richest Area in Texas

BRAZORIA COUNTY REVIEW

ING — Freeport—Velasco— West Columbia—Brazoria—Sweeny— Angleton—Rosharon—Danbury— Liverpool—Alvin—Damon—Clute—SERVING

ANGLETON, TEXAS, THURSDAY, MAY 29, 1941   10 Pages   NUMBER XII

Dobie Talks To Angleton High 1941 Graduates

ANGLETON—When I congratulate you, it is not only upon graduation but upon being from the country, said J. Frank Dobie, Texas historian, author and cattleman in his talk to the senior class Thursday night.

Culture isn't something you import, Dobie continued, it is something you develop out of your own soil, it is belonging. If you want to live positively instead of negatively, learn about your own environment for good comes from the things of the soil.

Following his theme of the strength of character and purpose developed by rural life, Dobie called to mind observances in the national defense program. Although New York, the greatest city in the world, would be the first to be attacked, few of its residents have volunteered.

More volunteers have come from Texas than any other state, and the rural south holds the best record of any section. "To fight is a virtue when war is necessary," the cattleman added.

The whole end of education is to teach you to size up a man, Dobie declared. He told several stories of his two favorite men in Texas history, Big Foot Wallace and John C. Duval, concluding with the sage comment that a lot of folklore should be in history and a good deal of history is folklore.

Dobie was introduced by J. P. Bryan. The senior class was presented by O. B. Robinson to E. E. Delaney who gave out the diplomas. "The Bells of Memory" was sung by a senior octet, Anita Stewart, Betty Jean Matthews, Jeanette Sheffield, Patsy Moseman, Robert Taylor, J. T. Holbrook, Melvin Coleman, Ross Baker, and Mary Beth Rucks, accompanist.

Surprise announcements of the evening where the faculty awards given out by Superintendent Wesley Edwards. Graduates receiving them were Elizabeth MacDonald, valedictorian; Ruth Perry, salutatorian; Roy Carr, high point boy; Ross Baker, citizenship; Betty Jean Matthews, activities and Anita Stewart, leadership.

ANGLETON—Mrs. David Spoor has returned to St. Joseph's in Houston and is seriously ill. She has undergone a second operation.

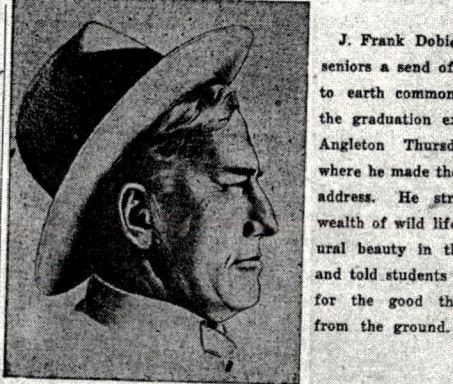

J. Frank Dobie gave the seniors a send off of down to earth common sense at the graduation exercises in Angleton Thursday night where he made the principal address. He stressed the wealth of wild life and natural beauty in the county and told students to search for the good that grows from the ground.

Attorney General Approves West Columbia's Bonds; Council Lets Equipment, Material Contracts

MANSFIELD EXPRESSES HOPE LABOR RACKETEERS WILL BE DISPENSED

ANGLETON—"I hope that a solution can be agreed upon and worked out by which labor racketeers will be entirely deprived of the power they seem to be exercising at this time," is the reply of J. J. Mansfield of the Brazoria County Development Association regarding strikes in national defense projects.

Mansfield says that he fully agrees with every word in the resolution and has repeatedly expressed the desire to have legislation proposed that would carry out these ideas. All bills covering these points have been referred to the judiciary committee Mansfield continues, and Chairman Sumners is in line with the view expressed by the association. However, the attorney general's office has claim that no further legislation is necessary and every branch of the government dealing with national defense seems to have discouraged the idea of any drastic legislation.

WEST COLUMBIA—The attorney general's approval of the water and sewerage bonds voted by West Columbia is now in the hands of Mayor Pat Pond and the city council. Bids have been let for the majority of the equipment and few more legalities stand in the way of the first day of actual construction work.

Pond says that he expects the approval of Chapman and Cutler bonding attorneys of Chicago in the next few days and a WPA work order within a week. Unless there is unforseen delay, work will start within 15 or 20 days after the work order is issued and both systems will be completed in about 10 months.

Layne-Texas company is drilling the water well on a bid of $5,400 and Pittsburg Des Moines Steel company is building the elevated tank and storage tank at a cost of $13,360. American Marsh pump company is installing $665 worth of equipment and Ludlon Valve Manufacturing company is putting in $3,000 worth of fire hydrants.

Man hole rings and other sewer equipment will be put in by Trinity Valley Iron and Steel company for $900. Cast iron pipes went to the National Cast Iron Pipe company for $13,782.

Fair Committee Chairmen Elected Thursday Night

ANGLETON—Chairmen were elected for a number of the important fair committtees at a meeting of the fair association directors Thursday night, and several days designated.

Mrs. G. E. Webb, Jr., was named chairman of the women's exhibits. This does not include the home demonstration division. Program chairman will be W. S. Dixon. Parade chairman is W. H. Pierce, and E. D. Brockman is auction chairman.

E. L. Coale will have charge of the carnival. It was voted that the carnival would not be permitted to charge a gate fee. Concession chairman will be J. R. Gayle, Jr. Others selected were E. L. Boston, first aid chairman; Brooks Hasty, lighting and electricity chairman, L. R. Johnson, police chairman and Howard Stewart, parking chairman.

All school children will be admitted free until six p. m. Friday and all negro school children until six p. m. Thursday. Friday was designated as school day and Thursday as negro day.

Officers and directors present for the meeting were J. S. Welboan, R. J. Higgins, Mrs. G. E. Webb, Mrs. George Sheffield, George W. Sheffield, W. C. Morris, H. A. Utley, E. H. Mays, Warren Moore, Miss Ora Slone, W. S. Millington and George Pearson. The next meeting will be in the courthouse June 26 at 8 p. m.

Review Advertisements Are Read by 5,000 People Every Week.

Freight Collides With Train Not Clear Of Siding In Angleton; Six Cars Derailed, Engine Overturned

66-Year-Old Engineer Jumps To Safety; Fireman Uninjured After Riding Train To Ground; Material Damage Heavy

The clash of steel, the deafening shrillness of a whistle, splinters of wood and sparks of fire filled the air and threw Angleton into a turmoil of excitement Wednesday night when the engine of a Missouri Pacific freight struck the rear end of a freight that had not cleared a siding, turning over the engine and derailing six cars.

A. Barnhouse, engineer of train 61 on the main track, jumped clear of the cab and received cuts and a large bump on his head. W. M. Jones, fireman, rode the train to the ground and came out with a cut elbow. The only other injury was a gash on the eyebrow of Roy Swansy, a spectator, who was running through the steam after the wreck and ran into a tree. Two women fainted during the excitement.

Although several railroad officials came immediately, they declined to make any statement. An unofficial explanation of the wreck indicated that the doubleheader with 85 cars, was shunted on the siding by engineers H. E. Ballard and L. W. Watson acting on dispatcher's orders. The brakeman signaled that the train was clear of the Angleton-Freeport highway and this signal was taken to mean that the train was clear on the siding.

It appeared however, that the last three cars were still on the main line when the train signaled all clear by dimming its headlight. The freight approaching from the east slowed from about 50 miles to 25 miles an hour but was unable to stop when the brakeman was seen signalling wildly with his light. The crash occurred at 8:36.

Barnhouse said that he had received a wire saying that the track would be clear at 8:25. He is 66 and has been on this run for 29 years. His train was running from Houston to Brownsville and the double-header was going from the Valley to Houston.

Damage was expected to run in the neighborhood of $12,000. All trains were routed through Rosharon until noon Thursday. The

Smith Sentenced To Fifteen Days, Is Fined $100

ANGLETON—A. J. Smith was fined $100 and sentenced to 15 days in jail in county court Wednesday. Smith pled not guilty to a charge of receiving and concealing stolen goods. He was convicted as a party to the metal theft at Dow.

The court gave the jury an instructed verdict Tuesday in favor of Archie Walker who was charged with transportation of liquor.

Butcher bond cases against James Green and Joseph Green were continued because of the absence of state witnesses. Joe Herman Hendry paid $100 and costs for carry aluminum knucks.

Angleton Has New Governing Body As Scouts Of Troop 37 Take Over City

ANGLETON — The honorable Henry Lee Sims is the new title of the scout who is mayor for a day when the boy take over the government of Angleton enforcing the laws and running the business.

Mayor Carlos Masterson has proclaimed Saturday as scout day for troop 37. Friday night, the heads of the departments will be

Blair Breaks Collar Bone, Jaw

FREEPORT—Henry Blair of Freeport received a broken jaw and broken collar bone in a wreck between Oyster Creek and Velasco early Saturday morning.

The other car driven by a man from Orange turned over but no

ANGLETON, TEXAS, FRIDAY, OCTOBER 25, 1940 — NUMBER 33

When County Fair Opened Tuesday

The snappy Angleton high school band is shown in top picture participating in the colorful parade which Tuesday opened the annual Brazoria County Fair and Fat Stock Show at Angleton, while in the bottom picture, left to right, are the following officers of the fair association: Richard Higgins, Angleton, secretary; B. M. Jamison, Angleton, vice president; J. S. Welborn, Freeport, president, and W. G. Stewart, Angleton, treasurer. Attendance on Tuesday and Wednesday each was in excess of 2500, and another big turnout was expected for today, school day. The fair is to continue through Saturday.

Fair Attracting Big Crowds To Angleton; Fine Exhibits Are Credit To Brazoria County

Parade Starts Event Off With A Bang Tuesday; Record Attendance Expected Today

ANGLETON.—Brazoria county is on display. The Brazoria County Fair and Fat Stock Show swung off in double quick time in Angleton Tuesday at 10 a.m. for a five-day exhibit. Backed by a claim of being the outstanding cattle raising and agricultural county of Texas, Brazoria ranchers, farmers, and homemakers proudly showed the best fruits of their endeavor in a setting of marching bands, carnival lights, and holiday spirit.

The parade, winding through bunting and flag-lined streets, was led off by the Legionnaires Tuesday. Following were the Angleton high school band, a detachment of the 69th Coast Artillery from Fort Crockett at Galveston, commanded by Capt. C. L. Partain, the Alvin, Sweeny and West Columbia bands, Liverpool, Freeport and Angleton Boy Scouts. On horses were cowboys and cowgirls, in cars the officials and guests.

Mayors Speak

When the gates to the grounds were opened, the speakers platform held the center of the stage. Here, a greeting was given by Judge O. K. Phillips and other addresses by E. C. Kimmons, mayor of Alvin; Truman Bown, mayor of Freeport; Pat Pond, mayor of West Columbia; Floyd Enlow, speaking for the mayor of Angleton, and J. S. Welborn, president of Brazoria County Fat Stock Show and Fair Association.

A big attraction was Captain Partain's detachment with anti-aircraft guns, a range finder, a sound detector, and a search light. Soldiers were very busy explaining the complexities of each to the crowd.

Horses, poultry, livestock and swine milled around their stalls showing off their carefully tended coats. Large and small, they were fine specimens of what Brazoria county can produce. The Future Farmers of America boys were there tending to their animals and listening to the praise.

Under a roof of moss were displayed the flowers, masses of blossoms, miniature arrangements, and single blooms. At the entrance was a lily pond and others lined the borders of the building.

(Continued on Back Page)

Two Producers In Rowan Field; Locations Made

Humble and Stanolind To Drill; Manvel Test Is Abandoned

Development of the new Rowan field southwest of Alvin on Chocolate Bayou continued this week with two producers being credited to the field and new locations being staked by Humble and Stanolind. Stanolind's Hodnett No. 1 was brought into production early this week flowing 200.71 barrels of 41 gravity oil over a 24-hour period on eighth-inch choke from 8527-42 feet. Gas-oil ratio was 221. Tubing pressure was 1,600 feet with 1600 pounds on the casing. Total depth of the well is 9006 feet. Rowan & Nichols No. 1 Bradbury appeared to have opened a deeper producing horizon in the field Thursday. The well was flowing distillate into tanks from perforations at 8964-74 feet. While a complete test had not been made late Thursday the flow was said to be running about seven barrels of distillate an hour through 3/16 choke, with an estimated gas flow of 1,600,000 cubic feet daily. A high gas pressure of 3200 pounds was freezing up in the separator. The rig is still in place and if production attempts are unsatisfactory at the lower level, it is likely the hole will be plugged back to the 8500-foot level.

Two Locations Made

Two new locations were made this week, with Humble having

Annabella, Visiting Here, Amazed To Find Such 'Marvelous Hotel in Such Small Town'

Actress Says Tyrone Power 'Lucky To Be Stationed at NATTC'

By JULIET KNIGHT

When a stir of excitement goes through the Officers' Club or a local restaurant, it is probably because someone has exclaimed, "Why, that's Annabella."

Heads are turned to see the blonde-haired French actress, who arrived here a week ago to visit her husband, Lt. Tyrone Power, USMCR, in training at the Naval Air Training Center.

This is her first visit to Texas, but, she added quickly, "I have crossed sections of the state before. It is very difficult to travel in the United States without crossing some part of Texas."

With motion picture parts in the West and stage roles in the East, her treks back and forth across the continent are almost as frequent as an airline pilot's. She knows this country almost as well as she knows her native France.

"Some say I commute between Hollywood and New York," she laughed.

Of all the things that animate her voice and the quick toss of her head, the theatre has the most spontaneous effect.

"I love it best in the world." The twisted position of her words give an added glitter to her conversation. "Every time I am ready to go on the stage, I am too nervous and scared, I say I will never do this again. Never again."

Asked whether opening nights do not always frighten great actresses, she held out both hands. "Being great, I don't know about, but being scared, yes."

"My great love is Helen Hays." She leaned forward on the couch, her feet curled up under her as she described the star of stage and screen. "Of all the actors and actresses, and all over the world, she is the greatest."

"When my husband and I get to New York, we go out of our minds," Mrs. Power said. "We get absolutely drunk with the theatre. Matinees every afternoon and plays every night."

The gray-clad ghost of the first wife in Noel Coward's "Blythe Spirit" puts in a mental appearance when Mrs. Power describes this, her favorite role. When she was on the stage against a gray curtain, the audience could see only her long painted nails, she was invisible to the cast, but her husband could see her distinctly.

"I was having so much fun when he made love to his second wife and he could see me there on the stage all of the time," she smiled mischievously. "I had a divine time."

The stage or a movie, she does not know which it will be next. When she leaves here in 10 days or two weeks, it will be to make arrangements for one or the other.

The drama of Mrs. Power's last tour was more significant than that of any put on by a stock company. The cast was all-star with five war heroes carrying the male rolls. Their appearances resulted in the sale of $32,700,000 worth of bonds.

It was an inspiration to Mrs. Power to be with the boys and she was impressed by the tales they had to tell as they crossed the country with her in an Army bomber. Referring to the work, she said, "We did it with all our hearts."

"After the tour, I came so far here to what I thought was such a little town. I found such a marvelous hotel that I was amazed. My husband is lucky to be stationed here," she added. "He loves it."

Another thing which a conversation with Mrs. Power brings to light is that her interest is intense in minor as well as major things. She eagerly surveyed the huge war industries which she has been shown in the last few weeks.

As much eagerness goes into her remarks about a motorboat ride on the bay or the taking of a picture. "I take pictures but they are all very bad. For some reason they turn out all black or all white."

There are so many expressions on Mrs. Power's face to watch, so many gestures to follow, that it would not be unusual for the person who was with her to notice last the clothes she wears.

When she was photographed in her apartment at the Robert Driscoll Hotel this week, she wore a green suit with a straight skirt, split at the sides. A scarf of white sequins finished the neck. Earbobs and a ring were gold discs with small red stones in the centers.

Her stay will be short here, but plans to return after she has ed her plans for the immed- uture. "My husband will be or some time, and you will back around," she prom-

MRS. TYRONE POWER
... Annabella

(Photo by Katheryn Pate)

Corpus Christi Women Who Joined WAAC Year Ago Have Wide and Varied Assignments

They left Corpus Christi during the last year wearing high heels, be-ribboned hats and dresses designed for their individual tastes. Now their uniform is regulation, their heels are sensible and their hats are no longer parked over one eye.

Aside from those obvious transformations, what has happened to the Corpus Christi women who enrolled in the WAAC? What advancements have they made and in what part of the country are they? These are some of the questions Lt. Martrine Armentor, local recruiting officer, set out to answer.

Their occupations are as varied as they were in civilian life, it was found.

One letter came from Betty Jane Truax, who was sworn in with the Clara Driscoll Platoon on Texas Independence Day. She is now at Officers' Candidate School in Des Moines. Her comment was, "We rise at 5:45 o'clock in the morning, fall into our beds exhausted at 9 o'clock at night, and we love it."

She's Sergeant Now

Closer to home is Geneva P. Harris who joined the corps the first of the year and is stationed at Ruston, La. Her job is that of railroad transportation clerk. Like father, like daughter, in the 1943 version, she has become a sergeant, a rank her father once held. He is W. F. Harris, master sergeant, USO, retired.

Lieutenant Armentor quotes a paragraph from a letter written by the sergeant to her father: "I like my work and feel now that I am a part of the war machine. I am so glad that I have a home and family to go to when it is all over. Many of the girls here are not so fortunate."

A mechanic and electrician who repairs airplanes is the classification of Auxiliary Maria A. Hinojosa who knew little about such useful arts when she enrolled March 7. She works in the state of the blue grass, her station being 165th Post WAAC Headquarters, Camp Campbell, Ky.

Like Overseas Caps

Auxiliary Florine V. Mathews after a 10-day furlough spent here, has returned to Camp Upton, N. Y., where she is in the motor-transport division. Her most enthusiastic comment when she reached camp was that "all the girls are now allowed to wear overseas caps and we love them for work." There is still nothing like a new style in millinery to cheer up a woman, be she civilian or WAAC.

Auxiliary Doris Katherine Kennedy is a chaplain's assistant. She is in her home state, stationed at Camp Hood.

Hard at work is Auxiliary Sara L. Prado who says she and another auxiliary are doing a four-person job. She has taken over the desk of a sergeant who is going on overseas duty. Her work is mimeographing, filing and general office jobs.

The last message came from Glenice M. Day, whose assignment is to bring more WAACs into service. Her station is in the WAAC recruiting office, San Antonio, and her rank, technician.

Fashion Expert Turns to Map Making as Member of WACs

July 22, 1943

Betty Truax Applies For Instructorship In Officer School

It was difficult for WAAC personnel officers to decide upon the capacity in which they could best use Betty Jane Truax. The Army had never had a category for fashion experts, and Miss Truax went into the corps after writing copy and selecting clothes for Glamor and Vogue Magazines.

When she received her third officer's bars this week, she had made up her mind where her military interest lies. It is in a Washington office making maps for Army use. Lieutenant Truax has applied for an instructorship in officer candidate school so that she can gain more experience in the map making field.

The lieutenant is the daughter of Mr. and Mrs. T. B. Truax, 212 Blevins Street, whom she is now visiting while on a 10-day leave. She was sworn into the corps here on Texas Independence Day with the Clara Driscoll Platoon.

Her basic training was received at Ruston, La., after which she was sent to officer candidate school at Fort Des Moines, Iowa. Her commission was received July 14. Her training for civilian employment had been at Traphagen School of Fashion in New York, and she was employed at the New York World's Fair for two summers.

In describing the discipline of the corps, Lieutenant Truax told of an incident when Robert Young, the movie actor, visited the school a short time ago. He accompanied officers on a barracks inspection. When it was completed, Young said, "That is the first time I have ever passed through room after room full of women without a one looking at me."

BETTY JANE TRUAX
... Commissioned

WAC Motion Picture To Be Shown Tuesday

August 8, 1943

HOTEL GREETERS FISH—Members of the local chapter of the Hotel Greeters of America made a fishing trip to the Gulf Friday as guests of Capt. Fred A. Coll on the boat Gracie E. Seated, left to right: W. A. (Bill) Cunningham, Howard Wright, and Jones F. Blanchard; standing: S. J. Hudson, Captain Coll, Richard Dalton, Joe Wolfsohl, Jeff Bell, Allen Marsden, and Jack DeForrest. Capt. A. W. Kurtz is seated at the wheel.

Gulf Fishing Trip for Local Hotel Greeters

Local members of the South Charter of the Hotel Greeters of America were guests of Capt. Fred A. Coll on the charter fishing boat Gracie E Friday for a fishing trip in the waters of the gulf and the bay.

Leaving before sunup, the fishermen made a short stop in Port Aransas then went into the gulf for deep water fishing. Capt. A. W. (Bill) Kurtz, former owner of the boat and now owner of Corpus Christi Courts, assisted Captain Coll in piloting the boat.

Making the trip were Allen Marsden, Nueces Hotel Manager and first vice-president of the greeters association; Jones F. Blanchard, owner of the Shoreline and secretary-treasurer of the association; W. A. (Bill) Cunningham, manager of the Robert Driscoll and chairman of the association board of directors; Jack DeForrest, Plaza manager; Howard Wright, Plaza auditor; Shelton J. Hudson, assistant manager of the Driscoll; Richard Dalton, night clerk and auditor of the Nueces; Joe Wolfsohl, manager of Jones Properties; and Jeff Bell, manager of the chamber of commerce.

Mexican Pilot Trained in States Makes Visit Here

June 3, 1944

Pablo Becerra, one of the four Mexican aviators to be chosen for U. S. Army Air Corps training in the 1942 CAA program, is spending the week in Corpus Christi visiting Lt. Jack Borden, instructor at NATC.

Becerra is now a pilot for Pan-American Airlines. He began flying in 1941 in private planes and came to San Antonio the next year with the first class of Central and South American aviators.

After training at Gardner and Randolph Field, he received his wings at Kelly Field, and took an instructors' course at Randolph Field.

He said that he refused the offer of a commission in the United States Army as he would be allowed to fly only as an instructor, and began making flights as a pilot of Pan American ships. Since that time he flown routes to United States ports of entry and Havana, accumulating 2,000 hours.

He has recently been recommended by Pan American as a pilot for the Airport Development Program in Mexico.

David Cohen, Bitter Foe of Isolation, Arrives in City

Dec. 19, 1943

"America has suffered from the illusion that she can be isolated, but it seems to me the only truly self-contained spots in the world are cemeteries," David A. Cohen, author of books and articles on widely varying subjects, said when he arrived in Corpus Christi yesterday.

"We have been trying to be in the position of the gal who doesn't want to marry the gent but doesn't want anyone else to marry him," he said. "And that can't go on forever."

Cohen began an attack on isolationism through the pages of the Atlantic Monthly with a series of articles in 1937, when he advocated using power to prevent the war instead of to fight it.

"Love in America," his most recent book, is a study of relations of men and women in this country. An aside was that he had a grand time writing it, for, as a bachelor, he could express himself.

One of the most serious and poignant questions of the time, that of the negro in American society, is attacked by him in next month's Atlantic. From his birthplace in the Mississippi Delta country comes his grasp of the problem.

Cohen is spending some time at the Robert Driscoll Hotel, coming here with Harry Benge Crozier, head of the Texas Unemployment Commission.

Index

A

agriculture, 61
Air France, 149
Alabama, 100
Alamo, the, 16
Alaniz, J. M., 140
alcoholism, 50, 63, 121, 142
Alps, the, 100
Alvin, Texas, 1
Alzheimer's Disease, 12
Anderson, Cap, 123
Angleton, Texas, 1–6, 7–9, 10–13, 14, 18–21, 63, 69, 132, 186
Angleton Times, 19–21
Anglican Catholic, 65
Anthony, Leigh, 105, 106
anti-Semitism, 18
Apalachicola Bay, 58
Apalachicola, Florida, 55
Aransas Bay, 56
Aransas Pass Progress, 168, 172, 183, 189
Aransas Pass, Texas, 55, 133
architecture, 140
Argentina, 117
Armstrong, Tom, 116
art, 106, 150, 183–185
Aruba, 67
Associated Press, 42
Atkins, Geoge, 21
Atkinson, Evelyn, 184
Atlantic Ocean, 149

Audubon Society, 57
Aunt Louise, 19–20
Austin, Texas, 14, 55, 100, 157
Avalero, Luis, 156
aviation, 21, 29–30, 71–74, 129
Ayling, Keith, 63

B

Bahia Marina, 174
Baker, Bobby, 121
Ballard, Jim, 23
Barnard, Bill, 41–42
Barnes, Al, 184
    Bob, 145–148
    Mary, 146
    Nanci, 184
Barrancabermeja, Columbia, 63
Basel, Switzerland, 100, 149
Bass, Perry, 169
Battle of Shiloh, 111
BBC radio, 30
Bean, Judge Roy, 27
Bedicheck, Roy, 14–15
Bee County, Texas, ix, 25
Beeville Bee-Picayune, 21, 22–24, 25–28, 29
Beeville Country Club, 23
Beeville, Texas, 22–24, 25–28, 29, 51
"the Beltway," *see* Washington, D.C.
Ben (program director), 68–69
Bermuda, 166
Bermuda onions, 166

Betts, Dennie, 109–111
Betty Boop Race, 174
Bexley, England, 152, 153
Bexley Heath, 152
Bexley Heath Station, 152
Bible, the, 15
Big Tree, 61
birds, 140
birdwatching, 57
Blackwell, Jack, 54
Blue Angels, 71
"Blue Baby" onions, 165
boating, 54–58, 99–100, 122–125, 126, 172–174
The Bobbsy Twins, 32
Bogotá, Columbia, 67
Boot Hill, 141
Booth, Herb, 184
bootlegging, 41
bordello, 102
Boring, Verle, 136
Brand, Othal, 166
Brazoria County Jail, 7–8
Brazoria County Review, 1, 18
Brazoria, Texas, 19
Brazos River, 4
Brill, Ida Nell "Nellie," 17
Broadway, 153
Brooks County, Texas, 140
Brother Leo, 113–118
Brown, Marg, 91, 110, 122–124, 186
Buckner, John, 147–148
Budd (announcer), 69
Buena Vista Ranch, 26
Burney, Cecil, 17, 93, 101, 160
Burns, Robert (poet), 155
Butt, H. E., 143
butter, wartime rationing of, 42–43
Byliners, the (writers' club), 52
Bynum, Kay, 52

C

cactus, 140
Calahan, 123
call-in radio programs, 88
Cambridge University, 15
Capital Press, 55
Capital Weekly Press, 100
Cartagena, Columbia, 66

Carlisle, John, 75–80
Carlsbad, New Mexico, 82
Casa Blanca (nightclub), 112
casinos, 56
cattle drives, 23
Centennial House, 114
Cessna, Ken, 95, 104, 105–106
Champagne, France, 187
Child Protective Services, 108
Chile, *see* South America
China, 101
Christ Church, 153
City Charter Commission, 138
Clute, Texas, 19
Clyde (announcer), 69
co-op advertising, 69
Coast Guard, 130
Coastal Bend, 164, 165
Coastal Bend Council of Governments (COG), ix, 138–142, 143–148, 159
Coastal Corporation, 127–128, 130
Cochran, Marilyn, 136
coconut, 66
COG, *see* Coastal Bend Council of Governments
Columbia, *see* South America
Common Cause, 84
Connally, John, 17, 129, 138
Cook, Andy, 134
Copper Canyon, 158
Corpus Christi, 2, 6, 17, 30, 32–37, 38–44, 45–47, 48–53, 54, 67, 73–74, 75–80, 88, 93, 101, 102, 117, 142, 187; Bay, 125; Chamber of Commerce, 91–92; Department of Public Safety, 75–76; firefighting force, 76; growth of, 33, 73, 125; Hurricane Celia and, 132–137; International Airport, 145; Marina, 124; Naval Air Station, 41; prosperity and, 125; shoreline, 41; southside, 159; waterfront development, 125
Corpus Christi Caller-Times, vii, 17, 30, 33–35, 38, 41, 42, 48, 57, 81, 160
Corpus Christi-to-Houston Yacht Club Regatta, 129, 130
Corpus Christi Transfer, 2
corruption, 25–28, 37, 87–88, 156

Costa, Joe, 93
Council of Governments' Environmental Quality Committee, 61
County Judges and Commissioners Association, 142
"Cousin Earl," *see* McBride, Earl
Covent Gardens, 151
Craine, Mrs. J. C., 141
Creveling, Jack, 125
crime, 11, 25–28, 33, 35–37, 75, 78
criminal justice system, 25–28
criminals, 8–9, 39, 41
Cronkite, Walter, 100–101
"The Crow's Nest" (newspaper column), 48, 52
Cuba, 107

D

Dale, Allan, 88
Dallas, Texas, 165
dams, 61, 127
Daughters of the Texas Revolution, 16
Davis, Louie, 102
Deen, Arthur, 15
Del Mar College, 138, 173
Del Mar subdivision, 111
Delaney, Lizanet, 4
Democratic Party of Texas, 101
Denton, George, 33–34, 43, 162
Dickinson, Emily, 146
district courts, 5
divorce, 56, 57
Dobie, J. Frank, 14–17, 23
dog run (house), 140
Driscoll Hotel, *see* Robert Driscoll Hotel
Duda (produce company), 167
dugout canoe, 64
Duhan, Joe, 6
"the Duke of Duval," *see* Parr, George
Dunn, Earl, 45–47, 68–69
Dunn, Joe, 75–80
Duval County, Texas, 111–112

E

East brothers, 114
East, Sarita Kenedy, 113–118
East Texas, 18

eco-tourism, 57
ecology, 8, 54, 59–62, 140, 141–142, 170
Edwardson, Delbert, 188
electronic journalism, 43
The Elms, 120–121
England, 15, 30, 32, 100, 135, 149–142, 170
English language, 156
Ennis, Vail, ix, 25–28
environment, *see* ecology
Environmental Quality Committee, 144
environmentalism, *see* ecology
Episcopaleanism, 65, 116, 151, 153, 188
Eton Chapel, 151
Eton, England, 150–151, 152
Europe, 149, 162
Evanston, Illinois, 93
Experiencing God (book), 188

F

Farenthold, Frances, 115
"the farm," 90, 95
FBI, 8, 33, 34, 35, 41, 160, 162
Federal Communications Commission (FCC), 86–90, 100
film techniques, 93
First Baptist Church (Corpus Christi), 80
fishing, 168–171
Flying Dutchman Juniors, 122
Flynn, Errol, 57
France, 41, 63, 149
Frank, Anne, 18
Franklin, Claude, 141–142
    Elaine, 141–142
fraud, 69
Freeport, Texas, 19, 20
Freer, Texas, 111
freeze plants, 55
Frio River, 180
Furley, Walter, 86, 89, 105

G

Galapagos Islands, 62
Galloway, Jack, 107–108
Galveston, Texas, 56
gambling, 56, 112
Gandhi, Mahatma, 117

Garrett, Harry, 54
Garrison, Quillian, 19–20
Gatwick Airport, 149
Germany, 18, 41, 42, 43, 163
Gertschow, George, 117
Getty, Buford, 187
Gibson, Fred, 17
Gill, Ruth, 147
Glazebrook, Connie, 114
Glusing, Ben, 140
Goldberg, Lazar, 162
Goldston, Jimmy, 124
Gone with the Wind (novel), 11
Goose Island, 61
Gravel Hill, 152
Great Depression, 1, 48, 112
Greek language, 106
Greek Orthodox Church, 106
Grosvenor Hotel, 150
Guadalupe River, 180
Guanajuato, Mexico, 157
Gulf Clipper (headboat), 124
Gulf Coast, 136, 172
Gulf of Mexico, 107, 114, 130
Gulf War, 128
Gunter, Dr. Gordon, 61–62
Guys and Dolls (stage play), 135

H

Hagar, Connie, 57
Hall House, 152, 153
Harney, John, 45–47
Hathaway, Jack, 23–24
Head, Hayden, 143–145
Heard, Nancy, 81–82, 83 (photo), 84–85, 137
Hebrew language, 163
Hedgpeth, Joel, 59, 60 (photo), 61–62
Heidi (book), 32
Henry VIII, 152, 153
Hermes, Doug, 22
Hispanics, 140, 145
Hobby, Oveta Culp, 101
Holiday magazine, 67
Holland, 122
Holy See, 118
Home Place (book), 17
horseback riding, 114
Hotel Kohler, 23

Hound Dog Man (book), 17
Houston Post, 12, 101
Houston, Sam, 16, 170
Houston, Texas, 1, 2, 7, 8, 12, 78, 100, 125, 127, 130, 131, 132, 146, 149, 187
Houston Yacht Club harbor, 131
Hug-the Coast Highway, 2
Hurricane Celia, 107, 132–137
Huson, Hobart, 140
Hussein, Saddam, 128

I

iguana, 64
Illinois, 110
Indian Point, 69
Indians, 64, 101
industry, 61, 126, 127, 128, 155–156, 167–171
Ingleside Cove, 124, 132, 135, 136, 137, 172, 173, 177, 181
Ingleside Index, 168, 172, 183
International News Service, 100, 102
International Society for the Prevention of Progress, 61
Internet, 169
Irish harp, 61
IRS, 166
Isle of Wight, 173
Israel, 160, 162, 166
Ivy League, 23

J

Jackson, Claudia, 173–174
 Robert M., vii–viii, 57
jade, 106
Japan, 21
Jews, 162, 163
Jim Wells County, Texas, 117
Johnson, Lady Bird, 121
 Lyndon Baines, 15, 17, 87, 101, 121
 Sam, 121
Joseph Jordan Knight home, 153
journalism
 advertising and, 2, 68–69; contacts and, vii, 104; ecology and, 61–62; electronic viii, *see also* KSIX, KZTV; follow-up stories, viii; industry and, 54–55, 81–82, 126, 128, 168–171; interviews, viii–ix, 22–23, 39; legal

Index 203

notices, 5; Linotype and, 19; local news, viii, 24; newspapers and radio/TV, compared, 38, 73–74; people stories, 12–13, 183–185; police reportage and, vii, 4–5, 7–9, 25–28, 34–37, 38, 41, 45–47, 104; public figures and, 17, 22–23, 25–28, 45–47, 75, 80; racism, 5, 25–28; reporters and, 48–83, 74, 75; rivalry in, vii–viii; small-town news, 1–2; standards and ethics in, viii–ix, 4, 22–23, 57, 70, 73–74, 100–102, 159–160, 186–187; UT School of, 1, 14, 15; women in, 38, 51, 81–82, 84; WWII and, 22, 24, 39, 41–44; *see also* radio, television
Junior League, 107
Justice, Theresa, 185
    Bill, 180
juvenile shelter, 109

K

Kansas City, Missouri, 93
Kansas City Star, 32
Katherine of Aragon, 153
Katz, Abe, 160, 161 (photo), 162–167
    Doris, 165, 166
    Leon, 163
    Max, 163
Katz building, 160
Keach, Sam, 159
Kenedy County, Texas, 114
Kenedy, Mifflin, 113
    Sarita, *see* East, Sarita Kenedy
Kenedy Ranch, 113–118
Kenedy Ranch case, 115–118
Kennedy, Kathleen, 99–100
    Mary (Whiteleff), 89, 100, 101
    Vann M., 69–70, 73, 86, 89–90, 92–93, 95, 96, 97, 98 (photo), 99–103, 119, 134
Kennedy, John F., 120
Kentucky, 32
KEYS, 133, 187
Khruschchev, Nikita, 120
King Air Jet, 166
King Charles, 150
King family, 113–114
King Ranch, 93, 116, 140
King, Richard, 113

Kingsville Record News, 106
Kleberg County, Texas, 140
Kleberg, Dick, 121
    Henrietta, 116
Knight, Ellen, 153
    Harriet, 153
    Hugh, 32
    Juliet, *see* Wenger, Juliet Knight
    Joseph, 153
    Launcelot, 2, 30, 31 (photo), 32, 35, 38, 54, 135, 157, 175, 176 (photo)
    Martha, 153
    Percy, 32
    Sue Taylor Thompson., 54, 67, 121, 175, 177
Knights of the Garter, 151
Kodak Brownie, 106
Kremlin, 120
KRIS-TV, 95, 139
KSIX radio, vii, 69–70, 71–74, 78, 88, 187
KSIX-TV, *see* KZTV
KZTV, vii, 89–90, 91–96, 97–103, 104–108, 109–112; 113–118, 187

L

Laredo, Texas, 101, 164
Las Vegas, Nevada, 23
law-enforcement officers, 7–9, 25–28, 33–37, 38, 45–47, 112
lawsuit, 57
Lay, Roy, 46, 102
Learning to Sail (book), 123
Lee, Bill, 15
    Lynn, 185
Left Bank, 183
Leica cameras, 43
Leo, Brother *see* Brother Leo
Leopard Street, 116
Lightcrust Dough Boys, 15
Lighthouse Restaurant, 117
Limbaugh, Rush, 88
Linkenhoger, Edgar, 87–88
Linotype, 18, 19, 186, 187
Lithuania, 162, 163
Lituanian lanugage, 163
Loch Lomond (Scottish Terrier), 177
London, England, 128, 150
London Zoo, 30
Long Island Sound, 128

204   News To Me

Looper, Gene, 86, 88, 90, 105, 133
Lord Fauntleroy, 30
Luby, Anna Maria, 111
   James O., 111
   James P., 111
   Mabel, 111
Luckie, Jo Ann, 173–174
"Lupe's Debutantes," 37
Lydia Ann Channel, 160

M

MacDuff (dog), 176 (photo)
Mack (printer), 19–20
Madison, Oliver, 11
Magadalena River, 66
Maginot Line, 41
Mamaronek, New York, 128
Mangold, Vera, 174
Mankof (produce buyer), 164
Maria (maid), 64
marine biology, 59
marine science, 100
Martineau, Paul, 110
Martinique, 117
Matamoros, Mexico, 102
Matthews, Tommy, 34–35, 41, 44
May Place Road, 153
Mayfair, England, 152
Mayflower (moving company), 2
Mc, Mrs., *see* McBride, Marguerite
McAllen, Texas, 166
McBride, Earl, 11, 12
McBride, Marguerite, 10–13, 19, 21
McClendon, Sarah, 119–120
McCracken, Bob, 48, 49 (photo), 50, 52–53, 54
McCracken, Dick, 53
McDonald, Ben, 128
McFarlane, Angus, 153
McGloin's Bluff, 136
McMullen County, Texas, 140–141
Menshemen onions, 166
Mera Lodge, 153
Mesquite Street, 48
meteorologists, 95
Metzger, Pearl, 120–121
Mexican consulate, 156
Mexico, 47, 121, 125, 155–158, 163–164
MG convertible, 106

Michael, Simon, 183
Michigan, 166
Midwest, 180
milo, 165
Model B Ford, 64
Monterrey, Mexico, 155–156
Moore, Henry, 39
the *mordido* (the bite), 156
Morgan, Wiley, 170
Moroles, Jesús Bautista, 185
Moulder, Mrs., 2
Mr. K, *see* Kennedy, Vann M.
Mulvany, Tom, 48, 50–52, 53
Municipal Coliseum, 110
murals, Mexican, 14
murder, 78
Mustang Island, 56, 61, 107
mynah bird, 186

N

National Cameraman's Magazine, 93
National Guard, 136
National Weather Bureau, 96
navy Intelligence, 41
Nazis, 162
NBC, 89
Negley, William, 169–171
Nelson, Jay, 180
Netanyahu, Benjamin, 162
Netanyahu, Jonathan, 162
the Netherlands, 122
New England Cafeteria, 53
New Orleans, Louisiana, 58, 93
New York state, 23, 128–129, 130, 164
The New York Times, 162
New York World, 93
Newhafer, Dick, 71, 72 (photo), 73
News Directors' Association, 187
911 emergency services, 131, 141, 182
Nixon, Richard, 128
Noname (boat), 174
North Beach, 102
North Shore, 168
Northwestern University, 93
Nueces County, Texas, 45, 52, 56, 140, 145

O

O'Daniel, Pappy, 15

Ocaña, Columbia, 65
Ocean Drive, 80
Odem, Texas, 39
Odom, Bob, 106
"Oh, Susannah" (song), 32
oil industry, 55-56, 81–82, 126, 128
Old Plot, 153
Old Stone Store, 141
Old Yeller (book), 17
Olé (boat), 172–173
"the Onion King," see Katz, Abe
onions, 164–166
Oppenheimer, Lady Helen, 150
    Sir Michael, 150
Ordner, Andrew, 76–77
Ortíz, Solomon, 145
Othello, 151
Oval Office, 120
Oxford, England, 151
Oxford University, 15

P

paddle-wheel boats, 64
Padre Island, 69–70
painting, *see* art
Palmetto Rancho, 111
Paris, France, 149, 183
Parker, Nancy, 63, 66, 67
Parr, George, 111
Parr's Pharmacy, 187
Patricia (dog trainer), 181
"People of the Bay Area" (column), 168, 172
Pete (itinerant printer), 20
photography, 41, 43, 95, 106, 134, 187
Pickford Road, 154
Pike, Leonard, 166
pink grapefruit, 140
Plaza Hotel, 78
pollution, 61
polo, 151
Pope, the, 57, 113, 115
Port Aransas, Texas, 41, 56, 107, 160, 173
Port of Corpus Christi, 145
Power, Annabella, 39, 40 (photo), 41
    Tyrone, 39, 41
Press Club, 124
Press Club Gridiron show, 188
Prince Charles, 151

Princess Margaret, 150, 151
Prohibition, 112
Protestantism, 65
Prouty, Bonnie, 185
Providence Place, 153
psychology, 188
Public Hall, 153
"Put Your Little Foot" (song), 23

Q

Quinn, Ellis, 22

R

racism, 5, 25–28
radio
    beginnings of, 68; fraud, 69; commercials, 68–69; Hurricane Celia and, 134; news coverage, 187; programming, 87, 88–89; virtues of, 71, 73; *see also* KSIX radio
Rainey, Homer Price, 15
Rancho Grande (nightclub), 112
Ray, Larry, 106
Rayburn, Sam, 101
Reynolds Metals, 107
Reader's Digest, 52
Red Cross, 106
Refugio, Texas, 140
Regnier, Carol, 174
    Keith, 174
Resource Conservation and Open Space Development Committee, 140
Rice, Rob Roy, 54–58
    Winnie, 56–58
Richards, Ann, 142
    Dick, 168J14
Richardson, Jean, 138
    Sid, 143
Rio Grande Valley, 88, 165, 166
Riviera Beach, 179
Robert Driscoll Hotel, 39, 41
Robstown, Texas, 90, 107, 164
Rockefeller Center, 42
Rockport Seafair, 173
Rockport, Texas, 54–58, 59–62, 132, 169, 183–185
Roman Catholic Church, 118
Roman Catholic Diocese of Corpus Christi, 114

Rome, 115
Ronstadt, Linda, 146
Roosevelt, Eleanor, 57
    Franklin Delano, 20, 43
Rotary Club, 41, 53
Rubáiyàt, the, 51
Runyon, Damon, 135
    Dick, 78
Russell, Steve, 185
Russia, 43, 163
Rusty (cabin boat), 55–56, 58

S

sailing, *see* boating
Saint George Castle, 151
Salinger, Pierre, 120
Saltillo, Mexico, 158
Salvation Army, 135
Sam Rankin Street, 37
San Antonio Express, 84, 100
San Antonio, Texas, 32, 41, 63, 82, 88, 100, 146, 162, 169,
San Diego, 112
San Francisco Bay, 62
San Patricio County, Texas, 107, 140
Sandy (polo pony), 52
Sarita, Texas, 114
"saucer and blow," 5
"String of Pearls," (song), 23
"Schottische" (song), 23
Schwartz, Buddy, 122
Scottish Terriers, 175–182
Scripps Institute, 61
sculpture, *see* art
Sea Sprite (boat), 172
seashells, 57
Seine, 183
Serendipity (sailboat), 128–130
Shah of Iran, 128
Shamrock Cove, 172
Shapiro, Roy, 165
Shell, Jack, 172
    Virginia, 172
Shemen, Ben, 166
shipyard, 55
Showroom building, 133
Shreveport, Louisiana, 91
shrimp cannery, 55
Simpson, O. J., 93

Sinclair Refinery, 128
"Sit Down, You're Rocking the Boat" (song), 135
slavery, 25–28
Smith, Farrell, 188
Sonya, Ontario, 64
Sotheby's Auction House, 151
South Texas, ix, 37, 61, 87, 96, 97, 107, 125, 126, 139–140, 155, 166
South Pacific theater of war, 54
South America, 52, 114, 118
Southern Comfort, 52
Southside Today, 159–160, 168
Southwestern Oil and Refining Company, 78
Soviet Union, 120
Spanish language, 156, 157
Speed Graphic (camera), 41, 187
Spunky (dogsitter), 177
Standard Oil Tanker, 67
Starboard I (dog), 177, 178 (photo), 179
Starboard II (dog), 17–180
Starboard III (dog), 180–182
State Department, 119
The State Observer, 101
"State of the Region," radio/TV show, 139–142
Steele, Fran, 132
stereotypes, 12
Stephenson, Coke, 55
Stone Age, 64
Storm, Wash, 117
Sweeny, Texas, 19
Switzerland, 149

T

Tampico, Mexico, 128
Tarleton, Dudley, 115
telephone service, 20, 23
television
    anchormen, 105; formative stages of, 91–96, 187; licensing by FCC, 86–90; police reportage, 104, 106, 109; reporters, 105–108; small-market station, 104; standards/ethics, 93, 95, 100–102; weather coverage, 95–96; *see also* KZTV
Texas A&M University, 166

Texas Grano 1015Y Supersweet onions, 166
Texas Hemisfair, 84
Texas history, revision of, 14
Texas legislature, 15, 169, 170
Texas Parks and Wildlife Department, 61, 169–170
Texas Produce Growers Hall of Fame, 166
Texas Ranger, 5
Texiana, 140
Thallman, Germaine, 149, 150, 151
Thames, 128, 151
Thomas, Helen, 120
Thomason, Dr. Robert, 68
Thompson, Paul J., 1, 21
Thornton, Girard "Thunder," 106–107
tidal wave, 133
tiger, 66
Tilden, Texas, 141
Tillery, Richard, 107
Tillman, Rich, 170
Time magazine, 65
Tontita (boat), 123–125
Tooker, Don, 106
The Toothache Tree (book), 108
"Tootie," *see* Luby, Anna Maria
Torah, 163
Toudouze, John, 82, 84
    Nancy Heard, *see* Heard, Nancy Sara, 85
trains, 20, 39, 157–158
Travis County, Texas, 142
Travland, Oscar, 29, 30
Trinity, 151
Truman, Harry, 146, 160
tuberculosis, 100
Tucker, Perry C., 2
Tulsa, Oklahoma, 89
"Tuxedo Junction," (song), 23

U

undulant fever, 6, 37, 68
U.S. Congress, 146
U.S. State Department, 128
U.S. Supreme Court, 52, 53
universities, English and U.S., compared, 151
University of Oklahoma, Norman, 93

University of Oregon, 61
University of Texas, 14–17; journalism school, 14–17; Library Tower dedication, 17; Marine Science Center, 61
uranium, 141
Urban, Larry, 128

V

Valley Onion, Inc., 165, 167
VE-Day, 62
VFW Hall, 169
Victor (diplomat), 156
Victor (truck drive), 3–4
Victoria (dog), 11–12
Victoria Station, England, 149, 150
Victoria, Texas, 129
Vienna, Austria, 100
Vietnam, 126
"Voice of Celia," *see* Cook, Andy

W

WACs, 101
Wall Street Journal, 117
Walnut Creek, California, 59
Walraven, Bill, vii–ix, 80
War Between the States, 113
Washington, D.C., 86, 119–121, 162
Washington, George, 162
Waterloo Station, London, England, 152
Watson (dispatcher), 35, 36
Weather Bureau, 12
Webb, Walter Prescott, 14–15
Wee Lass (boat), 173–174
welfare, 140
Weller, Bill, 124
Wells, Jim, 111
Wenger, Chris, 124–125, 126, 127 (photo), 128–131, 132, 133, 134, 135, 136, 137, 177, 178 (photo), 179–182, 183
Wenger, Juliet Knight
    in Angleton, Texas, 1–6, 7–9, 10–13, 14, 18–21, 69; at *Angleton Times*, 19–21; at *Aransas Pass Progress*, 168, 172, 183, 189; artists and, 183–185; aviation and, 21, 29–30, 71–74; in Beeville, Texas, 22–24, 25–28, 29–30; at *Beeville Bee-Picayune*, 22–24,

25–28, 29; bicycle and, 2, 3 (photo); boating and, 54–58, 99–100, 122–125, 172–174; at *Brazoria County Review*, 1–6; Brown, Marg, and, 91, 110, 122–124, 186; cancer and, 188–189; childhood of, 114, 157; with Coastal Bend Council of Governments, ix, 138–142, 143–148, 159; contacts and, vii, 67; in Corpus Christi, *see* Corpus Christi, Texas; at *Corpus Christi Caller-Times* (see *Corpus Christi Caller-Times*); at crime and accident scenes, 36–37, 78–80, 132–137; criminals and, 8–9; 36, 39; described, viii, ix, 10; Dobie, J. Frank, and, 14–17, 23; Dunn, Earl, and, 45–47, 68–69; ecology and, 57, 59–62; in England, 149–154; Ennis, Vail, and, 25–28; FCC hearings and, 86–90, 100; at first job, 1–6; fishing industry and, 168–171; geneology of, 153–154; Harney, John, and, 45–47; Heard, Nancy, and, 81–85, 137; Hurricane Celia and, 132–137; at *Ingleside Index*, 189; as interviewer, viii, 8, 39, 65, 77–78, 95, 106, 115–116; journalism school and, 1, 14–17; journalistic ethics/standards of, viii, ix, 4, 69, 70, 73–74, 120, 121, 137, 186–187; "juvenile delinquents" and, 6, 109–112; Katz, Abe, and, 160–167; Kennedy, Vann, and (*see* Kennedy, Vann M.); at KSIX radio, vii, 69–70, 71–74, 78, 88, 187; at KZTV (originally KSIX-TV), vii, 89–90, 91–96, 97–103, 104–108, 109–112; 113–118, 187; law-enforcement officers and, 7–9, 25–28, 33–37, 38, 45–47, 112; McBride, Marguerite, and, 10–13, 19, 21; McCracken, Bob, and, 48–50; Mulvany, Tom, and, 48, 50–52, 53; naiveté of, 1–6, 9, 102; Newhafer, Dick, and, 71–73; as news director, 73–74, 92, 94–96, 104–108, 187; on the "night side," 38–39; photography and, 43, 94 (photo), 134; Rice, Rob Roy, and, 54–55; in Rockport, Texas, 54–58, 59–62; at the *Rockport Pilot*, 54–58, 59–62; Scottish Terriers and, 175–182; in South America, 63–67; at *Southside Today*, 159–160; spirituality and, 113, 117; "State of the Region," radio/tv show, and, 139–142; television, training for, 93, 94 (photo), 95; undulant fever and, 6, 37, 68; in Washington, D.C., 119–121; Wenger, Chris, and (*see* Wenger, Chris); Wright, Buckley, and, 63–67

Welsh ballads, 61–62
West Columbia, Texas, 19
"West Wight Potter," 173
Winter, Bill, 149–152
Winters (criminal) 40–41
women in work force, 81, 87, 93, 147, 187–188
Wood, Lawrence, 140
Woolsey, Thomas, 152, 153
World War II, 18, 20–21, 22, 101, 162, 163, 165, 184; armistice, 30; crime and, 37; draft, 23, 36; end of, 44; prisoners of war, 42; rationing during, 20, 42–43; readjusting after, 45; women in, 21, 30
Wright, Buckley, 63–67
Wyatt, Bonnie, 131
   Doug, 126
   John Francis, 188
   Oscar, 126, 127 (photo), 128–131, 179

y

yachting, *see* boating
Young, John, 56

Z

Ziggie (housekeeper), 11